Autistic spectrum difficulties

IDENTIFYING AND SUPPORTING NEEDS • ACTIVITIES COVERING EARLY LEARNING GOALS • WORKING WITH PARENTS

HANNAH MORTIMER

Author
Dr Hannah Mortimer

Editor
Jane Bishop

Assistant Editor
Saveria Mezzana

Series Designers
Sarah Rock/Anna Oliwa

Designer
Rachel Warner

Illustrations
Ann Kronheimer

Cover artwork
Claire Henley

Acknowledgements
Qualifications and Curriculum Authority for the use of extracts from the
QCA/DfEE document *Curriculum guidance for the foundation stage*
© 2000, Qualifications and Curriculum Authority.

The publishers wish to thank Makaton Vocabulary Development Project for their help in
reproducing the Makaton illustration on page 56.
Every effort has been made to trace copyright holders and the publishers apologize for any
inadvertent omissions.

Text © 2002, Hannah Mortimer
© 2002, Scholastic Ltd

Designed using Adobe Pagemaker

Published by Scholastic Ltd, Villiers House,
Clarendon Avenue, Leamington Spa, Warwickshire CV32 5PR

Visit our website at www.scholastic.co.uk

Printed by Bell and Bain Ltd, Glasgow

5 6 7 8 9 0   4 5 6 7 8 9 0 1

British Library Cataloguing-in-Publication Data A catalogue record for this book is
available from the British Library.

ISBN 0439 98307 X

Autistic spectrum difficulties

KNOWLEDGE AND UNDERSTANDING OF THE WORLD

PHYSICAL DEVELOPMENT

CREATIVE DEVELOPMENT

PHOTOCOPIABLES

INTRODUCTION
Supporting children who cannot communicate can be both challenging and rewarding. This book aims to give you practical ideas about involving children with autistic spectrum difficulties within your regular group activities.

The aims of the series
A revised *Code of Practice* for the identification and assessment of special educational needs was issued in 2001, and this series aims to provide guidance to early years practitioners on how to meet and monitor special educational needs (SEN) under the Code. In addition, the QCA document *Curriculum Guidance for the Foundation Stage* emphasizes the key role that early years educators play in identifying needs and responding quickly to them. While most of us feel that an inclusive approach is the best one for all the children concerned, we still need guidance on what an inclusive early years curriculum might actually 'look like' in practice.

Within this series, there are books on helping children with most kinds of special needs:
- speech and language difficulties
- behavioural and emotional difficulties
- learning difficulties
- physical and co-ordination difficulties
- medical difficulties
- autistic spectrum difficulties
- sensory difficulties.

There is also a handbook for the whole series called *Special Needs Handbook*. This provides general guidance and more detail on how to assess, plan for, teach and monitor children with SEN in early years settings.

Many early years groups will at some point include children who have needs within the autistic spectrum. These needs cover a wide range of difficulties. There will be children who have been diagnosed with 'autism', 'Asperger syndrome' or as having 'autistic features'. Others might have 'pragmatic difficulties' linked to a speech and language disorder. Others still may have mild difficulties in communication and be rather stereotyped in their play and learning. In Chapter 2 (pages 15–24), you will learn what distinguishes each group of children. This book will help all early years professionals to recognize and understand such difficulties and to provide inclusive activities for the children concerned. Market research has shown that early years educators would welcome practical advice and guidelines for children with autistic spectrum difficulties.

How to use this book

Chapter 1 provides an introduction to your requirements under the revised *Code of Practice* for SEN as it relates to children who have autistic spectrum difficulties. This will be a brief guide only, with close reference made to the series handbook for more information. You will be reminded of the requirements of the QCA Early Learning Goals with particular reference to those in the area of Communication, language and literacy.

The need for individual education plans for those children who have SEN will be introduced and we will discuss what it means to meet SEN in an inclusive way. You will be given pointers for developing positive partnership and relationships with parents, carers and families. You will also be introduced to some of the outside agencies that you may be required to liaise with.

Chapter 2 looks more closely at the needs of children who have autistic spectrum difficulties. It considers what kinds of conditions and needs are covered in the book, how these difficulties arise and what you might notice among the children in your setting. It looks at what these difficulties mean for the child who is affected and what the educational implications are. It gives advice on how to look for special opportunities for promoting the development of communication skills, linked to the Foundation Stage curriculum. You will be encouraged to try a range of approaches and make use of the full range of resources and activities available in your setting.

Practical activities

Chapters 3 to 8 are activity chapters, each related to one of the QCA Areas of Learning: Personal, social and emotional development; Communication, language and literacy; Mathematical development;

Knowledge and understanding of the world; Physical development and Creative development. Each chapter contains ten activities, each with a learning objective for all the children (with or without SEN) and an individual learning target for any child who might have any one of a range of autistic spectrum difficulties. The activities will target different kinds of needs in the hope that early years workers will become able to develop a flexible approach to planning inclusive activities, dipping in to the ideas provided. It is suggested that you read through all the chapters for their general ideas, and then dip into activities as and when you need them as part of your general curriculum planning. As all children are unique, each activity will not suit every child with autistic spectrum difficulties. You may need to mix and match the general ideas to suit your particular situation.

Each activity includes a suggestion for the appropriate size of group, a list of what you need, a description of what to do, any special support that might be necessary for the child with SEN, ideas for extending the

activity for more able children and suggestions for links with home. Again, these guidelines should be used flexibly, guided by the needs of the children in your particular setting.

Although this book relates to the early years and SEN procedures followed in England, the general guidance on individual planning, positive behaviour management and activities will be equally relevant to early years workers in other countries.

How children's communication skills normally develop

At the age of six weeks, most babies begin to smile as they catch the eye of their parent or carer. This reaction brings such a warm response from the adult that communication flourishes and grows quickly. For

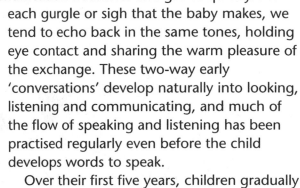

each gurgle or sigh that the baby makes, we tend to echo back in the same tones, holding eye contact and sharing the warm pleasure of the exchange. These two-way early 'conversations' develop naturally into looking, listening and communicating, and much of the flow of speaking and listening has been practised regularly even before the child develops words to speak.

Over their first five years, children gradually learn how to wait for a pause rather than to interrupt, how to share a topic of conversation so that both of you understand what is being talked about, and how to begin to see another point of view as well as their own. They gradually understand what communication is appropriate and what is not (for example, they come to know not to ask loudly and publicly, 'Why is that old lady crinkly, Mummy?'). These are complex and difficult skills to learn, yet most children will have picked up many of the rules of social communication by the time they start formal schooling.

Children with autistic spectrum difficulties

For some children, however, these normal communication and social skills do not develop spontaneously. Perhaps the child appears to be developing normally for the first year or so, but then communication and language skills seem to come to a halt. These children become more absorbed into their own worlds and agendas. They may use little eye contact, or even struggle to avoid it. They may join in an activity only if an adult insists and helps them, tend not to play with other children, and may seem aloof and indifferent to other people, preferring certain favourite objects, toys or videos. If they need something, they tend to lead an adult's hand towards it rather than to make requests.

Children with autism sometimes develop speech very slowly. Others may talk incessantly and be adept at remembering whole passages or rhymes. Their conversations, when they develop, can be one-sided, and the children find it hard to take on board the listener's point of view, talking about what is on their mind when the listener has no idea what it is. They may carry out little routines and rituals of behaviours in order

to 'keep the world the same', and they find changes to routines difficult to cope with. Their play tends to be repetitive and stereotyped, with little creativity or imagination.

As a generalization, children with autistic spectrum difficulties:
● have problems with social relationships
● find it hard to communicate
● experience difficulties with developing their imagination and play
● are resistant to changes in routine.

The term 'spectrum' reflects the wide range of difficulties that affect different children in different ways. At one end of the spectrum is a life-long disability that affects approximately 80,000 people in Britain, described as being 'autistic'. At the other end are mild autistic spectrum difficulties, where the autistic behaviours decrease as language and communication skills develop. Early diagnosis and help are vital in all cases.

Using resources

The activities described in this book encourage you to make use of a wide range of resources and materials, normally available in your setting. There are ideas for art and craft, story time, physical play, exploring and finding out. Special use is made of circle-time approaches with young children, since these have been shown to be effective in building their self-esteem and confidence and in teaching them how to join in and communicate within a group.

Research has shown that using a regular music circle-time can enhance looking, listening and confidence for children who have autistic behaviours, both within the circle time and beyond. Many of the activities presented in this book use a musical approach.

Links with home

All the activities suggest ways of keeping closely in touch with parents and carers. By sharing your ideas, you can play a role in helping the carers of a child who has autistic spectrum difficulties to follow approaches that will make everyone feel a lot more encouraged at home. If, in turn, you invite them to share their own expertise and knowledge of their child with you, you can make your teaching more carefully targeted for the child.

Providing special support

Make sure that the child with SEN is accessing the full range of your early years provision. Clearly, this cannot happen if the child is isolated in any way or withdrawn from the group regularly, and this is another reason for collecting ideas for inclusive group activities. 'Support' does not mean individual one-to-one attention. It means playing alongside a child or keeping a watchful eye so as to encourage new language and understanding, stay one step ahead of any learning opportunities and teach the child social skills in small groups. You will find suggestions for doing this in Chapter 2.

THE LEGAL REQUIREMENTS

This chapter explains your legal requirements towards children with autistic spectrum difficulties. There are ideas for planning and monitoring any special educational needs that these children may have, and for working with parents and other professionals.

The *Code of Practice*

The SEN *Code of Practice* is a guide for school governors, registered early years providers and Local Education Authorities, about the practical help that they can give to children who have special educational needs. It recommends that schools and early years providers should identify children's needs and take action, working with parents and carers, to meet those needs as early as possible. The aim is to enable all pupils with SEN to reach their full potential, to be included fully in their school communities and make a successful transition to adulthood. The Code gives guidance to schools and early years providers, but it does not tell them what they must do in every case. The contents of the new, revised SEN *Code of Practice* and are described in more detail in the handbook accompanying this series, *Special Needs Handbook*.

The *Code of Practice* principles

All young children have a right to a broad and balanced curriculum that enables them to make maximum progress towards the Early Learning Goals. Early years practitioners must recognize, identify and meet SEN within their settings. There will be a range of need and a range of provision to meet that need. Most children with SEN will be in a local mainstream early years group or class, even those who have 'statements of SEN' (see page 11). Parents, carers, children, early years settings and support services should work as partners in planning for and meeting SEN.

The *Code of Practice* is designed to enable SEN to be identified early and addressed. These SEN will normally be met in the local mainstream setting, though some children may need extra consideration or help to be able to access the early years curriculum fully. There is more detailed information about your requirements under the SEN *Code of Practice* in the series handbook.

Good practice can take many forms and early years providers are encouraged to adopt a flexible and a graduated response to the SEN of individual children. This approach recognizes that there is a continuum of SEN and, where necessary, brings increasing specialist expertise on board if the child is experiencing continuing difficulties. Once a child's SEN have been identified, the providers should intervene through Early Years Action.

Early Years Action Plus

When reviewing the child's progress and the help that they are receiving, the early years provider might decide to seek alternative approaches to learning through the support of the outside support services. These interventions are known as 'Early Years Action Plus', where 'Plus' characterizes the involvement of specialists from outside the setting. The Special Educational Needs Co-ordinator (SENCO) continues the leading role that they had under 'Early Years Action', working closely with the member of staff responsible for the child, and now also:

● draws on the advice from outside specialists, for example, early years support teachers, speech and language therapists or educational psychologists

● ensures that the child and their parents or carers are consulted and kept informed

● ensures that an individual education plan is drawn up, incorporating the specialist advice, and that it is included in the curriculum planning for the whole setting

● monitors and reviews the child's progress, with outside specialists

● keeps the Head of the setting informed.

For a small number of children, the help provided by Early Years Action Plus will still not be sufficient to ensure satisfactory progress, even when it has run over several review periods. The provider, external professionals and parents or carers may then decide to ask the Local Education Authority (LEA) to consider carrying out a statutory assessment of the child's special educational needs. The LEA must decide quickly whether or not it has the 'evidence' to indicate that a statutory assessment is necessary for the child. It is then responsible for

co-ordinating a statutory assessment and will call for the various reports that it requires from: the early years teacher (usually a support teacher, early years practitioner or LEA nursery teacher), an educational psychologist, a doctor (who will also gather 'evidence' from any speech and language therapist involved) and the social services department (if involved). It will also ask the parents or carers to submit their own views and evidence.

Once the LEA has collected the evidence, it might decide to issue a 'statement of SEN' for the child. Only children with severe and long-standing SEN go on to receive a statement – approximately two per cent of children in the United Kingdom. There are various rights of appeal in the cases of disagreement, and the LEA can provide information about these.

Requirements of the Early Learning Goals

Registered early years providers are also expected to deliver this broad and balanced curriculum across the six Areas of Learning as defined in the *Curriculum Guidance for the Foundation Stage*. This document has paved the way for children's early learning to be followed through from the Foundation Stage into National Curriculum assessment for school-age children. It was expected that the integration of these would contribute to the earlier identification of children who were experiencing difficulties in making progress.

The Early Learning Goals have been set into context so that they are seen as an aid to planning ahead rather than as an early years curriculum to replace 'learning through play'. Effective early years education needs both a relevant curriculum and practitioners who understand and are able to implement it. To this end, practical examples of Stepping Stones towards the Early Learning Goals are provided in the detailed curriculum guidance.

Within this book, each activity is linked to a learning objective for the entire group, and also to an individual learning target for any child who has autistic spectrum difficulties.

The activities presented in this book will also be relevant to the documents on pre-school education published in Scotland, Wales and Northern Ireland.

Individual education plan

Name: Jacob	**Early Years Action Plus**

Nature of difficulty: Jacob has mild autistic spectrum difficulties, with associated moderate expressive and receptive language delay. This means that Jacob is delayed in his communication, his social understanding, his speaking and his verbal understanding.

Action

1 Seeking further information

We need further information about autistic spectrum difficulties. Marie will contact the National Autistic Society and speak with Jacob's family or educational psychologist.

2 Seeking training or support

We will ask Michael, Jacob's speech and language therapist, to join us for a twilight session after pre-school to give all staff awareness training and leave us with reading material.

3 Observations and assessments

Marie will make regular observations of how Jacob's language and communication skills are coming on, and how he is playing with other children.

4 Encouraging social play and communication

What exactly are the new social and communication skills that we wish to teach?

Taking turns in play and conversations; eye contact; attention; ability to play socially.

How will we teach them?

● Marie will give Jacob five minutes of individual attention each session, during quiet time, looking through picture books, talking and holding two-way conversations, and carrying out activities aimed to improve his understanding of concepts, as advised by the therapist.
● We will say Jacob's name, touch his chin lightly and obtain eye contact before speaking to him.
● We will use physical activities to help him to develop 'reciprocal play' skills, for example, rolling and kicking a ball to another child, sending cars through a tunnel for another child to catch and return, and so on.

What opportunities will we make for helping Jacob to generalize and practise these skills throughout the session?

● Michael will write Jacob's speech and language targets in a diary that will come into pre-school with him. In this way, we can generalize the new skills that Jacob has been learning in the group.
● We will play alongside him when he is with another child to help him to communicate and play more socially.

How will we make sure that Jacob is fully included in the early years curriculum?

Each session, we will look for an opportunity to involve Jacob in a small group of two or three children, supervised by Marie, in which we can develop his social skills.

Help from parents

Jacob's mother will keep the diary going between home, group and therapist. She will meet with Marie for five minutes each Friday at home time to share progress and plan next week's activities.

Targets for this term

● Jacob will be able to point reliably to eight body parts when they are named for him.
● Jacob will look up when you say his name 20% of the time.
● Jacob will be able to play with another child on the train set for five minutes without help, sharing the game.
● Jacob will be able to hold a simple conversation with a familiar adult, using phrases of two to three words.

How will we measure whether we have achieved these targets?

Marie will do ten-minute observations during free play, once a week.

Review meeting with parents

Meet in half a term.

Who else to invite

Speech and language therapist.

The need for individual education plans

One characteristic of Early Years Action for the child with SEN is the writing of the individual education plan (IEP). This is a plan that aims to lead to the child making progress. An example of an IEP is shown on page 12, and there is photocopiable pro forma on the photocopiable sheet on page 85. This plan should be reviewed regularly with the parents or carers. It should be seen as an integrated aspect of the curriculum planning for the whole group, and should only include that which is additional to or different from the differentiated early years curriculum that is in place for all the children. You may find the section on 'Differentiation' in the series handbook helpful.

Case study: Jacob

Jacob is just four. His parents noticed that he did not start to speak at the same age as their friends' children. Their health visitor arranged for

specialist hearing assessments but these were normal. When Jacob was two, he was referred to the community speech and language therapist, who has been seeing Jacob and his mother regularly since. The therapist has found out that Jacob is delayed in both the understanding and expression of language, and he also has difficulties in understanding the other point of view, in holding conversations and in communicating socially with his peers. His behaviour tended to be repetitive and sometimes very stereotyped, lining up the same two cars in a certain order, or flapping his hands at the sides of his eyes. He was described as being 'slightly autistic' or as 'having autistic spectrum difficulties'. Jacob's therapist has been pleased with his progress, and has been keen to see him attend his local early years group where he can practise and enjoy his newly acquired words with other talking children. His needs are being monitored as Early Years Action Plus under the SEN *Code of Practice*, with ongoing advice and support from his speech and language therapist.

His early years teacher must therefore draw up an individual education plan at least every term, and meet with his parents and outside professionals regularly to review it. His therapist and parents also wish to see how his language and communication skills develop over the next year, as it is still possible that he might need a more specialist language unit placement once he is five.

Working with parents and carers

Parents and carers often ask how they can help at home when areas of concern are expressed by the early years setting. They might also approach you with their own concerns, which they need you to address with them. Parents and carers are the primary educators of their children and should be included as an essential part of the whole-group approach to meeting a child's needs from the start. They have expert knowledge of their own child, and you will need to create an ethos that shows how much this information is valued and made use of. Information-sharing is important and is a two-way process. There are practical examples of how you can involve the parents or carers in meeting their child's needs in the series handbook.

Working with outside agencies

When assessing and working with a young child who has SEN, an outside professional may be involved in helping the setting to monitor and meet the child's needs. For children with autistic spectrum difficulties, this is likely to be an early years support teacher, an educational psychologist, a speech and language therapist, a support team for autism or members of the local Child Development Team. The kinds of advice and support available will vary with local policies and practices.

Developing inclusive practice

'Inclusion' is the practice of including all children together in a setting, where the children all participate fully in the regular routines and activities of the classroom or playroom, even though these might need to be modified to meet individual children's goals and objectives. For this reason, the activities in this book carry both learning objectives for *all* the children (with and without SEN) and individual targets for the child who has SEN.

The factors that support inclusive practices and ideas for promoting inclusion for children who have autistic spectrum difficulties can be found in the next chapter.

HELPING CHILDREN WITH
AUTISTIC SPECTRUM DIFFICULTIES

In this chapter, you will read about some of the conditions that fall within the 'autistic spectrum' of difficulties and learn how you can support the children affected.

The conditions covered

Early diagnosis of any condition is important if children are to reach their potential, yet diagnosis of autism is rarely definitive. More usually, you will find that a child has been diagnosed with 'autistic spectrum disorder' or 'autistic features' rather than 'autism'. This is because there is a cluster of disorders, most of which appear to overlap.

In this book, the term 'autistic difficulties' is used to cover the whole spectrum of conditions. There is insufficient knowledge available about these disorders and how they relate to one another to be more specific. Experts still do not fully understand what causes autism, and there are many different theories. This chapter provides information about some of the most common conditions and theories, and some of the approaches that have proved helpful for children who have autistic difficulties.

Common problems

Children with autistic difficulties:
● find social relationships difficult
● usually have problems with communicating or conversing using words and gestures
● find it hard to play in a flexible or imaginative way
● can be very resistant to changes in routine.

Other children within the spectrum may have developed good language skills, but their social understanding remains very poor and they may show autistic behaviours. These children are sometimes diagnosed by a psychiatrist or psychologist as having 'Asperger

syndrome'. Children with Asperger syndrome and autism continue to experience difficulties as they grow older, and their conversation and communication tends to have an 'odd' feel to it and not to flow. Even as adults, they may have to work hard to remember social skills and to control their impulses to follow certain routines.

There are children who have difficulties in understanding language and in using it in a sociable way, or in understanding what is required of them in a social situation. These children are sometimes described as having a 'semantic-pragmatic language disorder'. They may receive help through a speech and language therapist. Their autistic-like behaviours tend to decrease as their language and communication skills develop.

As with all learning difficulties, there are bound to be children whose behaviours and learning styles fall mildly into the category of 'autism', but who have not been affected severely enough to receive help or diagnosis. You do not have to have a label in order to help these children. This book provides you with ideas to plan activities to help communication and social interaction for these children too.

The prevalence and causes of autism

We know that approximately 80,000 people in Britain today are described as 'autistic', and there are far more boys with autistic spectrum difficulties than girls. Many other people may be mildly affected by these kinds of difficulties.

Autistic people appear to see the world in a different way to other people. It might be that they inherited this difficulty (autistic spectrum difficulties can sometimes appear within families), or that their brains have developed slightly differently. It is most likely to be an interaction between many factors. Children with autism tend to focus on the details and parts of information rather than to see and understand the 'whole'. They also seem unable to understand what might be going on in someone else's head, making social situations frightening and unpredictable for them.

What you might observe

Children with autistic difficulties:

● often appear indifferent to other people and behave as if they were 'in a world of their own'
● may not play with other children and may only join in with activities if an adult insists and assists them
● sometimes indicate their needs by taking an adult's hand and leading them to what they want
● might have very little language
● may echo what is said to them
● might talk a lot about topics of great interest to them
● may become absorbed in arranging toys in a certain way, collecting certain objects, or spinning or turning toys repeatedly to watch them move
● might have poor eye contact
● may be unable to play imaginatively unless it is in a very stereotyped way
● might show bizarre or very fearful behaviour, especially if familiar routines are disturbed
● may be extremely good at some things, such as doing puzzles, identifying numbers, playing music or drawing.

What you can do to help

Appoint a key worker to the child who has autistic difficulties and help them to feel settled when playing one-to-one with this person. That worker can begin by simply playing in parallel to the child, observing how they are playing, placing new toys and objects of interest nearby, and gently leading the child when new instructions are needed (such as for outdoor playtime). As the adult becomes familiar with the child's routines and behaviours, it will become possible for that person to predict what the child will do next as they begin to see the world through the child's eyes.

Gradually involve one or more other children in the play, staying close to support and assist. Because you now have a feel of what the child will do, it will be possible for you to interpret the child's play to other children and thus include them in the play. You are acting as a 'bridge' for the child and helping them to grow into a more sociable person. You are also supporting the child so that they do not become fearful or anxious about the social situation. Social situations and other children's behaviour can be unpredictable and scary to a child who has no understanding of social rules and norms.

If the child understands language, use this time to talk about sharing, taking turns and understanding what other children might be thinking. Try to keep to a familiar and structured routine.

Children who have autistic difficulties find it hard to understand time sequences and sometimes become anxious about what will happen next. This makes it hard for some children to finish one activity since they are not sure how to start the next one. They might become 'locked' into very repetitive play in a bid to keep their world safe and predictable.

You can help by showing the child pictures or symbols about what is happening next (see page 36), making a series of cards with Velcro backs that can be arranged in line on a felt board, or by using a whiteboard to talk about and draw the session's timetable at the beginning of the day.

You can also help by suggesting appropriate words for what the child is doing, and by providing a simple commentary about what is happening, for example, 'John is building', 'Hettie is splashing' and so on.

Looking for special opportunities

Provide plenty of encouragement whenever the child communicates with you, whether they have done so with their voice or their actions. By now, because you have played alongside and observed the child, you will be familiar with their patterns of behaviour and communication. However, because they might use unusual signals and behaviours to indicate their need, you might have to put together a communication book to help other adults in the setting to understand the child, too.

You could start the communication book with details such as: 'This is how Abdul shows us that he is happy'; 'This is how Tom shows us that he is uncomfortable'; 'This is how Sara shows us that she is thirsty'; 'This is how Lee shows us that he needs the toilet' and so on.

Sometimes children with autistic difficulties have intense interests in certain items or topics, for example, they might be fascinated by trains and tracks, or very interested in switches and electrical things. They might cling on to two oblong bricks and stare at these intently as they arrange them meticulously in line, or they might insist on carrying a certain blue beaker everywhere.

Be aware of the child's interests, but introduce new things to them as well. For example, add cars to the train mat, help the child to extend their fascination in bricks to building and simple construction play, and provide a special place to put the cup that the child carries everywhere so that their hands are freed up to play with other things. Try to support their activities, but aim to distract them if they become too absorbed or obsessed with certain things.

Children with autistic difficulties are often thought to be deaf, because they pay little attention to spoken instructions. In order to communicate with the child, use their name clearly, physically get down to their level, try to establish eye contact, and then speak. Give very clear and simple messages, showing the child as well as telling them what to do.

For children who are severely affected, try the following approach. Spend ten minutes a session playing alongside the child with another of the same toy or piece of equipment. Copy what they are doing. When they begin to notice what you are doing, move in to play with them, sharing the same toy. Again, copy their actions. The idea is to encourage the child to see that their behaviour is resulting in your behaviour. Next, begin to play turn-taking games, for example, blowing bubbles for the child to burst (see page 25), setting up and knocking down skittles (see page 74), shaking a 'slinky toy' between you so that you can each feel its movement (see page 79) or rolling a musical toy to and fro (see page 80). The idea is that the child will begin to see your company as useful and fun.

Removing distractions

Provide a quiet safe base where the child can go if they are feeling over-loaded or stressed. Children with autistic difficulties quickly feel stressed and anxious if there are many people about or if the demands on them

are too great. If there is too much stimulation of any kind, they might revert to repetitive movements or play just to make the world predictable again.

Once you have got to know the child, you will be able to see when they are feeling stressed and to encourage them to move to the quiet area to 'wind down'.

You may find that the best thing to do is to reduce the number of options and to play with just one toy or activity at a time, putting all other materials well out of sight. For example, you could start to build a jigsaw with just the last three pieces missing.

In order to give the child the idea that there is choice, show them two activities or toys and ask them to touch the one that they want to play with next. Use physical prompts such as hand-over-hand support or a light touch to encourage success in what the child is doing, then praise them strongly to reward them on successful completion. At first, you might need to pair this with something more concrete, such as a burst of music from a tape, a musical box or a small piece of fruit, as some autistic children do not respond to social praise alone.

Being patient

You may need to wait longer than usual before a child who has autistic difficulties responds to what you have asked for. They sometimes need longer than other children to process what you have just said or shown them before they can put together their response. Give the child time to respond or to imitate before you ask again or give an answer. In addition, by pausing for a response, you are providing an expectancy and a 'tension' for the child to do something in return. Make sure that it is clear to them what you expect them to do, perhaps by showing as well as telling. Aim to use a few clear words and say the same words consistently, for example, 'Please, sit down'. If you reword your instructions or add explanations and detail, it can quickly confuse the child.

Sometimes Makaton signing is used in order to make instructions and requests clearer (see page 96), or children are taught to exchange pictures or symbols in order to make their needs known more clearly. You may find some of the activities in the other books from this series helpful, especially those from *Behavioural and Emotional Difficulties* and *Speech and Language Difficulties*, both by Dr Hannah Mortimer.

Children with autistic difficulties often have problems in understanding personal pronouns such as 'me' and 'you'. It is helpful to use real names, for example, 'Give it to Molly' rather than 'Give it to me'. They also find it hard to understand question words such as 'what' and 'why' and sometimes may provide rather unusual and irrelevant answers to questions. The speech and language therapist may help the child step by step towards understanding more abstract words, and you could follow these ideas, too.

Encouraging early language

In order to help children with autistic difficulties to communicate with you, encourage them to show you what they want. Sometimes, make it a little bit difficult for them to get what they want so that they learn to communicate at whatever level they are capable of. If a child can simply get a drink by climbing on the cupboard and helping themselves, what need has that child to communicate? But if you anticipate what they want and offer a simple choice, then you are expecting them to point or reach for their choice. This is a very early stage of communicating that can be developed.

Later, you can expect the child to make an approximation of the word 'drink' such as 'di'. Try using this approach before rough and tumble play, too, as many children with autistic difficulties love physical play. If you wait until you have the briefest of eye contact with them before starting it, you will have taught them to begin to communicate what they want.

Children with autistic difficulties sometimes love music, so you could aim to use music time to encourage them to look, listen and join in. Many of the activities in this book use music to encourage participation from the children. You might also find the 'Music Makers' approach (see page 95) a useful way of planning activities for all the children, which are also precisely targeted for the child who has learning difficulties such as autism.

Looking for structure

Children with autistic difficulties can find it hard to cope with free play. When there is no clear structure, they might begin to behave inappropriately or retreat into repetitive or rigid behaviours. Consider trying to introduce some structure for these children, even to free playtimes.

Organize or direct the child's play if you can, and stay close to support and suggest ideas. Offer clear choices of what to play with next, and make sure that the child has some favourite toys and activities within the choice. You might find it necessary to actually teach the child how to play with different toys in order to build up the repertoire. A play checklist such as *Playladders* (page 96) provides a useful aid.

Trying different approaches

There are many approaches for supporting people with autism. The following are the ones most widely used in early years settings and in parent programmes.

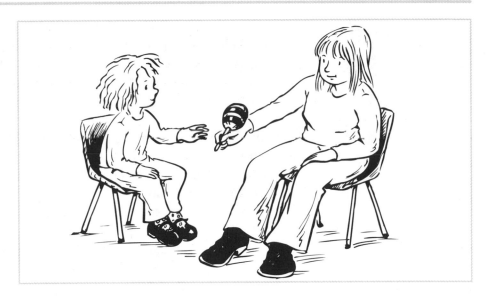

TEACCH

TEACCH stands for 'Treatment and Education of Autistic and Related Communication Handicapped Children'. This approach was developed in North Carolina, USA, and is often recommended by professionals for use in settings in the United Kingdom. It uses structured teaching, cuts down on the words used and makes the most of visually presented information. It can help children with autistic difficulties to make sense of their surroundings, predict what will happen next, understand how events are connected, and so become more independent and less frustrated.

By following the TEACCH approach, you would make clear visual boundaries for the child. The 'red table' might be where they did their early writing and number, and it might be screened off from other play activities such as sand and water, so that the child had few distractions. Visual timetables would show them the sequence of activities and events that session. They might have a 'finish box' for placing completed pictures or puzzles in, so that they know clearly when it was time to move on. They would be shown how to do everything rather than simply be told. While you might not want all the children in your setting to be quite so structured and restricted in their play, these approaches have been shown to be helpful for children with autistic difficulties. The activities in this book will help you to plan approaches using some of these ideas.

Intensive Interaction

'Intensive Interaction' is a way of learning about people and communication. It is based on how babies and carers learn naturally to respond to one another and takes the child who has autistic difficulties back to this early stage of learning to communicate. It relies on mutual enjoyment of an activity, imitation, physical contact and a gentle running commentary. The adult uses bursts of activity followed by a pause to create an expectancy that the child will respond. Rhyme, rhythm and timing are made use of with the adult watching and waiting for a response. In this way, a child can learn how to behave in a reciprocal way ('My turn, your turn'). Again, you will find that many of the activities in this book are borrowed from these approaches, particularly those using musical interaction as a first step towards early conversations and verbal communication.

Gentle Teaching

'Gentle Teaching' was developed as a non-aversive approach for helping people with learning difficulties. It avoids using approaches that might feel punishing or aversive and uses rewards and ignoring instead. Because children with autistic difficulties are often highly anxious and easily stressed by other people or social contact, this approach has become popular in early years settings. The central strategy is to ignore or interrupt an inappropriate behaviour, then to redirect the child on to something more appropriate, then to reward that new behaviour.

Daily Life Therapy

In 'Daily Life Therapy', children with autism work intensively in groups. Dr Kiyo Kitahara believed that these children have weak emotions causing a disruption to their behaviour and learning. Children are taught to conform to 'normal' behaviour and development using highly predictable routines. Many of the activities in this book make use of routines and predictability to help children with autistic difficulties to join in and feel more secure.

Parent programmes

Parents or children with autistic difficulties will also need advice and guidance on caring for their children. There are various parent programmes available, here are details of some of them.

Portage

Some children who have been diagnosed early with autistic difficulties might have been receiving help through a Portage home visiting service before the child joined your setting. Portage was first introduced to this country in the late 1970s at a time when parents would have traditionally been taking their child along to a child development centre for assessment, therapy and 'expert advice'. Parents found themselves having to relate to many different professionals, and their own expertise and detailed knowledge of their own children was not being harnessed to the full. There are now Portage home teaching services throughout the United Kingdom and beyond.

Registration and validation of training are co-ordinated by the National Portage Association (see page 96). During Portage assessment, there is a regular, usually weekly, visit to the home by a trained home visitor. A shared assessment framework, usually the Portage checklist, is used, which draws on the child's development to establish a profile of strengths and needs. There is a programme of teaching activities

tailored to the needs of the individual child. There follows positive monitoring of the child's progress with regular review. Management and advisory support for the service is provided by a team composed of representatives from all the contributing agencies and the parents or carers. Ask the parents to share the Portage checklist with you so that you can celebrate the progress already achieved by the child and continue to teach them step by small step.

The EarlyBird Programme
It was originally set up by The National Autistic Society in 1997 to develop and evaluate a model of early intervention for children with autism, using a parent programme. It is a three-month programme that combines group-training sessions for parents with individual home visits. Video feedback is used to help parents to apply what they have learned on the course with their children at home. It aims to support parents in the period between diagnosis and the start of school, to empower them and help them to facilitate their children's communication and appropriate behaviour at home, and to help parents develop good practice in handling their children. The approach used incorporates elements from the Hanen Program, the SPELL approach, techniques from the TEACCH approach and the Picture Exchange Communication System (PECS).

All the approaches mentioned in this chapter may be of interest to early years practitioners working with young children who have autism, and further information can be obtained through The National Autistic Society (see page 95). The Society also has information about the various interventions that have been used to work with children with autism, though not all have been fully evaluated.

The Hanen Program
The Hanen Program trains parents and carers to assist with their children's early language and communication skills through a series of teaching sessions, activities and observations. There is a book available for parents entitled *More Than Words: Helping Parents Promote Communication and Social Skills in Children with Autistic Spectrum Difficulties* by Fern Sussman (see page 95). This book is also very helpful for settings as it explains how to observe and communicate with a child who is still at the early stages of making their needs known and interacting with others. Some of the ideas from this approach have also been built into the activity chapters in this book.

The Lovaas Approach
This approach, developed by Dr Lovaas, uses intensive behaviour modification techniques with children who have been diagnosed early with 'autism'. Most of the children follow intensive programmes at home during their pre-school years (perhaps 40 hours a week of one-to-one intervention for two to three years).

The aims are to reduce inappropriate behaviour or any behaviour that interferes with learning, and to teach absent skills in a structured way in order to help the child to develop and learn. 'Normal' behaviour is expected and any 'autistic' behaviour tends to be ignored. In this way, it is argued, the child comes to learn through the systematic use of rewards and prompting how to behave like any other child.

In your setting, you can best prepare yourselves by studying the programme that the child is on and asking questions to the parents or carers and Lovaas therapists. Find out what precisely the goals are for the time that the child is with you, what rewards and ways of encouraging them have been effective in the past, and when help from an adult should be given and what form it should take. This should help you to work out how the programme can be delivered effectively, yet unobtrusively for the other children, and how you can include the child fully in your activities, making best use of the shadow worker's support. If you need more advice on managing difficult behaviour, you will find the publication *Developing Individual Behaviour Plans in Early Years Settings* by Hannah Mortimer helpful (see page 95).

The Options Approach

In the 'Options Approach', constant individual attention is provided by the parents or carers and adult volunteers in order to help the child to establish relationships. It begins with a Family Programme course to introduce the approaches to the parents or carers. It is suggested that if adults accept and enthusiastically interact with autistic children at their level, the children will respond and become less isolated. These children tend to be educated in their own playrooms by adults who imitate and warmly approve of all their play and behaviours, keeping them relaxed and encouraging much greater responsiveness.

PERSONAL, SOCIAL AND EMOTIONAL DEVELOPMENT

The activities in this chapter provide ideas to help children to develop their social skills and to concentrate. Children with autistic difficulties find these skills particularly difficult.

LEARNING OBJECTIVE FOR ALL THE CHILDREN
● to form good relationships with their peers.

INDIVIDUAL LEARNING TARGETS
● to improve eye contact
● to develop reciprocal play.

Feeling bubbly

Group size
An even number from two to eight children.

What you need
A jar of bubble-blowing solution and a wand for each pair of children.

What to do
Wait for a dry day and take the children outside. Gather them around you and show them how to dip a wand into the bubble solution and how to gently blow a bubble. Ask the children to find someone else to be their partner. Give the bubble-blowing kits out to each pair of children and encourage them to share. Ask them for ideas about how they will do this: will they each have three blows or do they want you to tell them to swap every couple of minutes? Praise them for thinking of good ideas and support them as they use these.

When the children have enjoyed sharing the bubble mixture for five minutes or so, suggest that as one child blows, the other should chase and try to 'pop' the bubbles.

Finally, encourage the children to move around the outdoor space while you blow plenty of bubbles. Invite them to chase and pop the bubbles, and praise them for not bumping into one another!

Special support
Children with autistic difficulties are often fascinated by bubbles. They love to see the round shape growing as a bubble is blown, they enjoy chasing and popping the bubbles. This activity encourages them to look closely at their partners' faces and to anticipate the next bubble. Stay close to the child that you are targeting so that you can encourage them to make a sound or a gesture to 'ask for' the next bubble from their partner. They will probably prefer watching to blowing.

Extension
Let older children experiment with different strengths of soap solution and different-shaped wands. Which works best?

LINKS WITH HOME
Give each child a bubble set to take home and ask parents and carers to play the blowing-and-popping game, taking turns with their children.

LEARNING OBJECTIVE FOR ALL THE CHILDREN
● to be confident to try new activities, initiate ideas and speak in a familiar group.

INDIVIDUAL LEARNING TARGETS
● to make choices
● to indicate a preference.

I like it!

Group size
Two to four children.

What you need
An A3 copy of the photocopiable sheet on page 86; sheets of card; paper; pens; glue; scissors.

What to do
Sit down with the children and show them the pictures on the enlarged photocopiable sheet. Explain that each picture shows one of the things that the children can do in the group. Encourage the children to identify them and talk about each picture in turn. Ask them questions such as, 'When do you have your drink?' and 'When do we go outside?'.

Help the children to cut the pictures up and share them out. Ask them to help you by colouring them in. Mount each picture on a piece of card with glue. Now invite the children to tell you whether you need more pictures. What else do you do in the group? Ask for their suggestions and add some more illustrations, then colour and mount them.

Special support
Use these cards to make a 'choice board' for a child who is still at the earliest stages of communication. Put up a few choices to begin with (including 'toilet', 'drink' and a favourite activity) and by sticking them to a low notice-board. Encourage the child to touch or point to the picture to show you what they would like to do next.

Extension
Read *More Than Words* by Fern Sussman (Hanen Centre Publication) to find out how to use visual helpers to extend a child's communication and to help them to learn to behave more socially and appropriately.

LINKS WITH HOME
If this approach works well, suggest a simple choice board for parents and carers to use at home as well. You could also make a simple book or laminated sheet to be shared between home and your setting.

Now you see me

Group size
Ten to 24 children.

What you need
A light chiffon or silk scarf.

What to do
Invite the children to sit in a circle on the floor. Crouch in the middle and ask a confident child if you can cover their face for a moment while you teach everyone a new game. Place the scarf lightly over the face while you sing this song to the tune of 'Frère Jacques' (Traditional):

> *(Abdul)*'s hiding! *(Abdul)*'s hiding!
> Where is he? Where is he?
> *(Tara)*'s going to find him! *(Tara)*'s going to find him!
> All say 'BOO'! All say 'BOO!'
>
> *Hannah Mortimer*

Sing the children's names, choosing a second child to approach 'Abdul' and pull away the scarf as everyone calls 'BOO!'. Now let Tara and Abdul change places. Let Abdul put the scarf over Tara's face before he sits down. Choose another child to pull the scarf off. Continue with the game until everyone who wants a turn has had one.

Special support
This simple game is useful for anticipation and eye contact. Start by playing 'Peep-bo' with the child that you are targeting on a one-to-one basis. Then include them in the circle so that they can watch what is happening. Then support them as they pull the scarf off another child's face, and encourage them to look that child in the eye and say, 'BOO!'. Stay close as they wear the scarf, and do not force this at all if they are frightened.

Extension
Adapt the song into a 'Hide-and-seek' game with one child hiding and the other seeking.

LEARNING OBJECTIVE FOR ALL THE CHILDREN
● to maintain attention, concentrate and sit quietly when appropriate.

INDIVIDUAL LEARNING TARGETS
● to make eye contact
● to develop confidence when interacting with others.

LINKS WITH HOME
Encourage 'Peep-bo' games at home and explain to parents and carers why they are so helpful for a child at the early stages of looking and communicating.

LEARNING OBJECTIVE FOR ALL THE CHILDREN
● to work as part of a group.

INDIVIDUAL LEARNING TARGET
● to develop confidence when sitting close to other children.

Pass the parcel

Group size
12 to 30 children

What you need
Two small boxes; sticky tape; wrapping paper; musical tape or CD; tape recorder or CD player; adult helper.

What to do
Wrap the boxes securely in attractive wrapping paper, sticking the paper well down. Choose some lively music and ask your helper to be in charge of the tape recorder or CD player.

Invite the children to sit in a circle and ask if they know how to play 'Pass the parcel'. Explain that this game is a bit different because the children will not actually open the parcel; instead, you will tell them to do something. Ask them to pass the parcels around when the music plays, and to stop when it stops. Show them which way to pass the parcels.

Give a few children at opposite sides of the circle a parcel each and start the music. After ten seconds or so, stop the music and see who has the parcels. Encourage the children to call out the names of the children with the parcels and ask these children to change places. Start the music again and continue the game, swapping places until everyone is sitting next to someone completely different. At the end, ask some of the children to 'introduce' their neighbours to you.

Special support
Sometimes children with autistic difficulties find it hard to accept other people close to them. Use cushions or carpet squares to 'mark' places in the circle if this is easier. Sit close to the child that you are targeting to reassure them.

Extension
Give each child in the circle a name of a colour, a flower or a form of transport. Play some music. When it stops, ask, for example, all the 'reds', all the 'roses' or all the 'buses' to change places.

LINKS WITH HOME
Sometimes it can be helpful if the parent or carer of the child that you are targeting sits close to their child in the early stages of settling into your large group. Invite them to stay for circle time or music time if this would help.

PERSONAL, SOCIAL & EMOTIONAL DEVELOPMENT

LEARNING OBJECTIVE FOR ALL THE CHILDREN
● to work together harmoniously.

INDIVIDUAL LEARNING TARGET
● to accept the close proximity of a partner playing in parallel.

Copy cat

Group size
The child that you are targeting.

What you need
Two sets of identical play equipment.

What to do
Choose the child's favourite activity, such as the train set. Place yourself beside the child so that if they raised their head they would see you. Watch how they are playing and pick up identical pieces of track and engines so that you are mirroring their play. As they roll their engine backwards and forwards, do the same. As they make train noises, so do you. Follow them as they move around the room, mirroring them whenever it is appropriate to do so. Repeat this for about ten minutes each session.

In time, the child might begin to look up from time to time and notice what you are doing. As you continue with the sessions, the child might begin to look up to see whether you are still copying. At this stage, you have helped the child to move from solitary play to 'playing in parallel'.

Special support
This activity is suitable for children who behave as if they were 'in a world of their own' and who are still at the earliest stages of taking notice of other people.

Extension
Once you are beginning to play in parallel together, begin to share the same toy, perhaps pushing the train to and fro between you. Try to encourage 'reciprocal play' together, which involves turn-taking. Then begin to introduce another child into the play.

LINKS WITH HOME
If this approach is proving helpful, ask the parents or carers to spend five minutes a day mirroring their child's play at home.

LEARNING OBJECTIVE FOR ALL THE CHILDREN
● to be sensitive to the needs and feelings of others.

INDIVIDUAL LEARNING TARGETS
● to give indirect eye contact
● to play alongside another child.

Mirror magic

Group size
The child that you are targeting.

What you need
A large (preferably wall) mirror; two teddy bears.

What to do
Invite the child that you are targeting to sit or kneel down in front of the mirror, then do the same, so that you are side by side. At first, allow the child to explore the reflections and note whether they seem to be aware of their own reflection or not. Try placing their hands up to the mirror. Try stepping out of sight and then saying 'Boo!' as you reappear in the mirror. You may need to spend a few sessions playing in front of the mirror until the child is used to reflections.

When the child has begun to look at you in the mirror, start to play a game with a teddy bear. Give the child a teddy and hold one yourself. Say, 'Teddy UP!' as you raise your bear high and encourage the child to imitate with the movements or the words, or both. Continue with 'Teddy DOWN!', then add your own variations, making it fun for the child to copy you. Take a turn copying the child's movements as well. Keep the session very short to begin with and build up the time as the child learns to watch and to copy for longer.

Special support
This activity is helpful for teaching children with autistic difficulties to copy. Once children can copy, they can begin to join in action songs and also to learn from each other's play.

Extension
Other children can play this game in pairs, facing each other. Encourage them to take it in turns to be the leader, so that the other child mirrors everything that the leader does.

LINKS WITH HOME
Ask the parents or carers to sit at a mirror with their child and to point to noses, heads and so on saying, for example, 'Daniel's nose, Mummy's nose'. Advise them to use real names instead of 'my' and 'your'.

LEARNING OBJECTIVE FOR ALL THE CHILDREN
● to take turns and work as part of a group.

INDIVIDUAL LEARNING TARGET
● to develop confidence within a larger group.

Mad hatter

Group size
Eight to 20 children.

What you need
A box full of hats (a police helmet, firefighter's helmet, sun-hat, scarecrow's straw hat, space helmet, soldier's beret, surgeon's paper hat and other assorted hats); musical tape or CD; tape recorder or CD player; wrapped box (perhaps one of the parcels from the activity 'Pass the parcel' on page 28).

What to do
Place the box of hats in the centre of the floor and ask the children to sit around it in a large circle. Explain that they should pass the parcel around when they hear the music, showing them which way to pass it.

Play the music for approximately 15 seconds. When it stops, see who is holding the parcel. Invite that child to go to the box and choose a hat. Whisper to them as you help them to choose someone to pretend to be. Perhaps they are going to put on an old cap and mime being a fisherman, or they are going to be a soldier and mime 'exercises', or even a firefighter putting out a fire with a hose. Ask the rest of the group to guess who the child is pretending to be.

Continue until several children have had a turn.

Special support
Children with autistic difficulties often find it hard to think imaginatively. Sit close to the child that you are targeting so you can encourage them to look and listen. Give them a choice to help with their guess, for example, 'Is it a policewoman or a soldier?'. When they choose a hat, suggest a simple action for them to mime.

Extension
Encourage older children to mime the different roles without the added clue of the hat.

LINKS WITH HOME
Some children with autistic difficulties will not tolerate hats on their heads, even in winter. Playing with hats in your group can help them to get used to them. Include the child's winter hat from home in your selection.

LEARNING OBJECTIVE FOR ALL THE CHILDREN
● to respond to significant experiences.

INDIVIDUAL LEARNING TARGET
● to make eye contact when greeted.

Pleased to meet you

Group size
Six to 24 children.

What you need
Just the children.

What to do
Use the greeting song below at the beginning of group time or circle time. The aim is to greet each child by name, and encourage a look, a smile, a wave, or even a 'joining in' from very confident children. Let the children choose how they are going to respond, and do not expect them to sing or speak to you unless they feel ready to. It is advisable to sing this song unaccompanied so that you can move around the circle and vary the speed. If you have adult helpers in the circle, tell them that they must sing too to keep you company!

Move around the circle so that you can look each child in the face at their level. If a child has poor visual attention, give a touch on the shoulder or leg to engage their attention.

Sing to the tune of 'Tommy Thumb, Tommy Thumb, Where Are You?' from *Round and Round the Garden* (Oxford University Press).

> Callum Browne, Callum Browne, Where are you?
> Here I am, Here I am, How do you do?
>
> *Hannah Mortimer*

Put the child's name into the first line. If you prefer to use just first names, sing 'Hello, Callum, Hello, Callum' instead. If you have a very shy child who hides their face, sing 'There he is, there he is' so that he is still included.

As the children get more familiar with this greeting, encourage them all to wave at the child being greeted. This will help them to learn each other's names. Shake hands or touch a foot for the last line.

Special support
Sometimes children with autistic difficulties find it easier to sing a greeting than to cope with speaking and all the uncertainty of the social exchange. If they enjoy it, sing this greeting song for certain children as they come in to your setting.

Extension
Older children should be able to remember every child's name and could sing the greeting song as they move around the circle.

LINKS WITH HOME
Send a photograph home of the children in the setting, together with a piece of paper giving all their names. Ask parents and carers to help their children to name all their friends.

Full circle

Group size
Eight to 12 children.

What you need
A carpet square for each child.

What to do
Sit down in a circle together. Make it easier for younger children by placing carpet squares in a circle for them to sit on. Older children can hold hands in a circle and then sit down.

Ask the children to show you their fingers. Can they wiggle them? Can they put all their fingertips together like this? (Show them how they can touch their left-hand fingers with their right-hand fingers.) Now can they touch fingers with their neighbour? Help them to form pairs around the circle as they put both sets of fingertips together.

Now ask them questions such as, 'Can you touch your nose?', 'Can you touch your friend's nose?', 'Can you touch your elbow?', 'Can you touch your friend's elbow?' and so on.

Once you have warmed up in this way, pass a gentle touch around the circle. Touch the foot of the child sitting next to you. Encourage them to 'pass' that touch to the next child by touching their foot. Send different touches all around the circle and praise the children for being gentle.

Special support
Sit next to the child that you are targeting so that you can prompt their responses.

Extension
Make up a spoken version of this game by passing a sentence around the circle. Find further ideas in the book *Circle Time for the Very Young* by Margaret Collins (Lucky Duck Publishing).

LEARNING OBJECTIVES FOR ALL THE CHILDREN
● to maintain attention and concentrate
● to form good relationships with adults and peers.

INDIVIDUAL LEARNING TARGET
● to accept and pass on a gentle touch.

LINKS WITH HOME
Ask parents and carers to play a game with their children at home to teach body parts, using a soft toy and asking questions such as, 'Can you touch Teddy's nose?'.

Goodbye song

Group size
Eight to 20 children.

What you need
Just the children.

What to do
Use the 'Goodbye' song below at the end of circle time or music time, or at the end of a session as the children go home. Sit in a circle and sing the song to each child as you encourage a look, a wave or a smile from them. You can dismiss each child from the circle as you all sing 'Goodbye' to them. Have a helper or two on hand to encourage the children who are leaving the circle to move to the next activity, such as snack time.

The tune is the first two lines of 'Twinkle, Twinkle, Little Star' (Traditional). Substitute the child's name in the second line. Move around the inside of the circle as you sing a verse to each child in turn.

> Now it's time to say 'goodbye',
> *(Sammy Lee)*, off you fly!
>
> *Hannah Mortimer*

Touch each child lightly to dismiss them, or shake hands as another variation. You will need to use some sort of physical prompt to let them know when they can 'fly', or they will be tempted to leave before they have looked at you and made their goodbyes!

Some children (regardless of need) might like to come with you on your journey around the circle, and do the shaking hands or waving with you. Encourage the child that you are targeting to help you in this way from time to time.

Special support
Children with autistic difficulties sometimes find it hard to finish one activity and start another. Always make sure that the child that you are targeting knows where to go and what to do next.

Extension
Older children could lead this activity with your encouragement.

LEARNING OBJECTIVE FOR ALL THE CHILDREN
● to respond to significant experiences.

INDIVIDUAL LEARNING TARGETS
● to give eye contact when saying 'goodbye'
● to signal 'goodbye'.

LINKS WITH HOME
Encourage parents and carers to wait out of sight until you are ready to sing the song, as children with autistic difficulties may find it distressing to wait once they have seen their parent or carer arrive.

34

COMMUNICATION, LANGUAGE AND LITERACY

These activities encourage early language and literacy skills and will help children with autistic difficulties to communicate more clearly. This is an area that these children may find especially difficult.

LEARNING OBJECTIVE FOR ALL THE CHILDREN
● to read a range of familiar and common words and simple sentences independently.

INDIVIDUAL LEARNING TARGETS
● to look at a picture and comment on it
● to read familiar and personalized words.

LINKS WITH HOME
Involve parents and carers in choosing the photographs as they will know what really interests their children. Ask them to sit with their children and read through the book together, pointing at the words as they read. In time, their children may begin to remember the phrases and link them to the pointing.

My own book

Group size
One child at a time.

What you need
Sheets of coloured A3 sugar paper; white paper; scissors; glue; photographs (see below); stapler (adult use).

What to do
Make an individualized 'first reader' for the child that you are targeting, or to encourage any child to enjoy early reading.

Lay six sheets of different-coloured sugar paper on top of each other, staple them across the centre and fold them in two to make an A4-size book. Collect together a series of photographs relating to each child doing different activities in your group, their family and friends, their home and pets, and their favourite toys and occasions. Involve each child in choosing what to photograph if they are capable of helping you in this way.

Sit down with the each child in turn and show them the blank book. Suggest that you fill it with words and pictures for them to read and look at. Spread out the photographs and let the child choose ones that mean something and that interest them.

Decide together which photographs you are going to put in the book first, then help the child to stick them. Ask what writing the child would like on the same page, such as 'Holiday Dad'. Extend this into a simple sentence for the child, for example, 'I went on holiday with Dad', and write this on a piece of white paper. Cut it out and glue it beneath the photograph. Build up the book page by page over several sessions. When it is complete, read it together over and over and talk about the pictures.

Special support
If the child does not have words yet, let them choose the photographs, then add a single-word caption beneath it, for example, 'Mummy' or 'Rex'. Choose single words for your captions if a child is younger or still at an early stage of using language.

Extension
Invite older children to make up and write their own captions.

LEARNING OBJECTIVE FOR ALL THE CHILDREN
● to use talk to organize, sequence and clarify events.

INDIVIDUAL LEARNING TARGET
● to use visual helpers as an aid to understanding.

Helpful pictures

Group size
One child at a time.

What you need
Cards; coloured pens; Blu-Tack; display board.

What to do
Use this activity with any child who finds changes in routine difficult and who would find it hard to cope with a visitor coming in to join you or a similar event.

In advance of such an event, sit down with the child and talk about what is going to happen. Draw a picture to represent each stage of what will happen in order to provide something concrete for the child to understand. For example, if you are expecting a visit from a fire engine and a team of firefighters, you might draw pictures such as the ones below:

Stick the cards on to a display board in order, from left to right. Go over the pictures again and rehearse the ideas with the child.

Special support
With the activity 'Copy cat' on page 29, you read about using visual helpers to offer a child choices. In this activity, you are using them to help a child with autistic difficulties to understand the events in the day and how to cope with new routines. You will find more ideas in the book *More Than Words* by Fern Sussman (Hanen Centre Publication).

Extension
Invite older children to think through events in their days, draw picture cards and add their own captions.

LINKS WITH HOME
If parents and carers are finding a particular event at home difficult to deal with, help them to use this kind of approach with their children.

LEARNING OBJECTIVE FOR ALL THE CHILDREN
● to use language to re-create experiences.

INDIVIDUAL LEARNING TARGET
● to talk about their day when looking through their personal communication book.

LINKS WITH HOME
Ask each child's parents or carers to talk through the book with their child so that they are in touch with what they have been involved in at that session. Suggest that they continue it at home and send it in for you to share with the child during the next session.

My day

Group size
One child at a time.

What you need
A small notebook; coloured pens.

What to do
This activity is aimed at a child who has difficulties in communication and requires you to compile a record book. Observe the child throughout the session and write a 'personal story' about what the child has done. Write about the child in the third person, for example, 'Scarlett painted today' or 'Cian played with the train'. Write from the child's point of view so that you are only including events in which the child was actually present. Describe what people did and said in that situation, for example, 'Mrs Baker said "That's lovely, Joshua" and she put it on the wall'. Finally, give the child something to try to do or say in the situation, for example, 'I wonder where George hid his boots, next?'. Add simple illustrations. Try to write a few pages a day of two to three lines with pictures on each page.

Just before the end of the session, sit down with the child and read through your book, looking at the pictures together and talking about the story.

Special support
Children with autistic difficulties find it hard to understand time sequences and to tell their parents or carers about their day. This book uses visual aids to prompt the child to remember what happened in their recent past.

Extension
Older children can write and illustrate their own personal stories.

LEARNING OBJECTIVES FOR ALL THE CHILDREN
● to link words to pictures and sounds to letters
● to extend their vocabulary.

INDIVIDUAL LEARNING TARGET
● to name action words.

Name it!

Group size
Four to six children.

What you need
An A3 copy of the photocopiable sheet on page 87; card; crayons; scissors; glue.

What to do
Show the children the enlarged photocopiable sheet and explain that all the pictures are about actions. Ask them to tell you what Teddy is doing. Help them to think of the words for running, sitting, lying, jumping, falling and drinking. Cut the pictures up and give one to each child to colour in or over. As you work together, encourage the children to think of the letter sound with which each of these words begins. Ask questions such as, 'Has anyone got a word beginning with "s"?' or 'What sound does "jumping" begin with?'. Mount the pictures on cards with glue and place them on one side to dry.

Later, sit together in a circle on the floor. Turn the cards upside-down. Challenge a child to turn over the cards one at a time until they find the action that begins, for example, with 'r'. Turn them back and challenge the next child with a new sound. In time, the children will be able to remember where the card they are looking for is.

Special support
For children with autistic difficulties, learning action words is sometimes one of their targets. When it is their turn to turn over the cards, encourage them to find the 'running' teddy or the 'sitting' teddy (and so on) to keep the task simpler for them.

Extension
Ask the children what sound all these words end with. Can they think of more action words and draw more cards for the game?

LINKS WITH HOME
Tell parents and carers which action words you are teaching their children and ask them to find opportunities to say and use those words at home.

Puppet party

Group size
An even number from two to eight children.

What you need
A glove puppet for each child and one for yourself.

What to do
Gather the children together and introduce the puppets, one by one. Pass them around and invite the children to give them characters and make them move. Explain that the puppets are going to play a copying game. Let each child wear a puppet. Make your puppet move in a definite way, for example, curling up or waving. Encourage all the other puppets to copy. Now take it in turns for different puppets to take the lead while the others copy. Continue until each child who wants to has had a turn. Then help the children to choose a partner, and ask one puppet to copy the other until you ask them to change over. Finish with a general dance for the puppets before they all wave 'goodbye'.

Special support
This activity encourages reciprocal play and imitation skills for a child with autistic difficulties. The advantage of this activity is that the child is taking turns with another child rather than an adult. Stay close to encourage turn-taking. Even if the child finds it hard to copy, they might still notice the other child copying them. Sometimes puppets make interaction less direct and are therefore easier for a child with autistic difficulties to use for communication.

Extension
Use the puppets to teach a simple sign language such as Makaton (see page 96).

page 96).

LEARNING OBJECTIVE FOR ALL THE CHILDREN
● to explore and experiment with sounds and words.

INDIVIDUAL LEARNING TARGET
● to communicate indirectly with another person.

LINKS WITH HOME
Encourage parents and carers to use puppet play at home if their child has autistic difficulties.

LEARNING OBJECTIVE FOR ALL THE CHILDREN
● to use language to imagine and re-create roles.

INDIVIDUAL LEARNING TARGET
● to communicate indirectly with another child.

Hello, goodbye

Group size
Six to ten children.

What you need
Two toy telephones.

What to do
Sit down in a circle together and show the children the toy telephones. Pick up the receiver and dial a number. Then tell one of the children, 'It's for you!'. Encourage the child to lift the receiver as you pick up yours. Say, 'Hello? Who's there?'. Encourage the child to say their name. Ask them a simple question such as, 'Did you walk to group today?' or 'What colour are you wearing today?'. Develop this into a simple conversation. Then ask the child which of their friends in the circle they would like to telephone next. Say, 'Goodbye' and put down your receivers. Pass your telephone to the friend and encourage the first child to dial and the friend to answer. Support the children as a new telephone conversation develops.

Special support
Sit beside any child that you are targeting and keep the conversation simple, encouraging them to say their name and to listen between bouts of speaking. Some children with autistic difficulties find it hard to stop speaking long enough to allow the listener to reply – this should be supported and encouraged. Others will tend not to speak, but might be encouraged to say 'hello', 'goodbye' or their names.

Extension
Use old, real telephones in the role-play area and encourage simple conversations as part of a game of 'Offices' or '999'.

LINKS WITH HOME
Ask parents and carers to find an opportunity for their children to develop real telephone conversations with a favourite relative or friend.

LEARNING OBJECTIVE FOR ALL THE CHILDREN
● to link sounds to letters, naming and sounding the letters of the alphabet.

INDIVIDUAL LEARNING TARGET
● to match letters.

Matching words

Group size
Two to six children.

What you need
Coloured plastic letters (such as magnetic letters); card; coloured pens; scissors.

What to do
Prepare for this activity by choosing some simple words that you would like the children to learn. These might be because they have a high personal meaning to the children (such as their names) or because they are keywords in their early reading books. Gather the plastic letters that make up the chosen word and lay them on a piece of card. Draw around them in the same colour as the plastic letters, then colour in the letter outlines so that you have identically coloured words on your card. Cut the card letters out. Repeat on a second piece of card, but this time using a black pen and not colouring in the outline.

Challenge the children to match the letters to the card letters. At first, give them just the coloured cards and the appropriate letters to match on to them. Later, use your cards with the black outlines and introduce more choice in the letters. Encourage them to say the letter sounds as they place the letters, then to read the whole word back to you. Ask them what other words they would like you to make with them.

Special support
Some children with autistic difficulties are interested in letters and love matching tasks such as this one. Stay close to say the letter sounds to them as they place each letter into position.

Extension
Encourage older children to help you to prepare this task, building up the words and drawing around the letter shapes.

LINKS WITH HOME
Make the outline of each child's name and send it home with the component letters. Ask the parents or carers to help their child to match the letters and to read their name.

LEARNING OBJECTIVE FOR ALL THE CHILDREN
● to link sounds to syllables.

INDIVIDUAL LEARNING TARGET
● to listen and anticipate.

Train game

Group size
Eight to 20 children.

What to do
Sit down together in a circle and tell the children that you are going on a pretend train journey. Say that you are going to have your dinner on the train, but it is a very funny dinner because it is back to front! Ask the children to copy what you do and say what you say.

Chant these words to sound like a steam train gathering momentum. Churn your arms like the pistons on the wheels. Start very slowly and quietly, then get louder and faster as the chant gathers momentum.

> Cof-fee, cof-fee,
> cof-fee, cof-fee,
> Cheese and biscuits, cheese and biscuits,
> cheese and biscuits, cheese and biscuits,
> Chocolate pudding, chocolate pudding,
> chocolate pudding, chocolate pudding,
> Fish and chips, fish and chips,
> fish and chips, fish and chips,
> *SOOOOOOOOOOOOOOOUP!*
>
> *Hannah Mortimer*

As you reach the last line, hold up your arm as if you were sounding the steam whistle. Repeat this a second time, now that the children know what to expect. Then stand up and make a long train as you chug around the room, chanting the verse.

Special support
Use your tone of voice and your actions to hold the attention of the child that you are targeting, and pause fractionally for them to anticipate the final 'Soooooooooooooooup!'. If they find it difficult to form a long train, allow them to move independently when you stand up until they are more used to this activity. Then encourage them to take a turn at being the 'engine', with the other children following behind.

Extension
Go to your book corner and make up a similar chant using book titles or story characters (perhaps ending with 'Spoooooooot!').

LINKS WITH HOME
Send copies of the photocopiable sheet on page 88 home with the children to use as they chug up the stairs to bed with their parents or carers.

What is in the box?

LEARNING OBJECTIVES FOR ALL THE CHILDREN
● to extend their vocabulary
● to use talk to clarify ideas.

INDIVIDUAL LEARNING TARGET
● to develop an understanding of simple abstract concepts.

Group size
Six to ten children.

What you need
A small and pretty box with a lid that fastens; selection of small items to fit inside the box, such as a baby's dummy, comb, spoon, seashell and small car.

What to do
Place one of the items in the box and hide the others near by. Ask the children to sit down in a circle. Introduce the box and peep inside without showing the children what is in it. Invite them to pass it around the circle but not to look inside. As the box passes around, sing the song below to the tune of 'Girls and Boys Come Out to Play' (Traditional):

> What is in the box today?
> Pass it round but don't you look!
> What is in the box today?
> *Let's ask* (Jacob) *to take a look!*
>
> *Hannah Mortimer*

When you reach the last line, add in the name of the child who is just about to receive the box and stop while the child takes a peek inside. Move close to the child and support them as they describe what they can see, such as, 'It's for your hair... it's long... it's brown'.

Help the child to find words to describe the object without actually naming it. They may find this difficult at first, but it will become easier with practice and will really make them think. Continue the activity with other items from your selection.

Special support
Children with autistic difficulties often find abstract language particularly hard. This activity is suitable for a child who has developed expressive language, but they will still need your help. They will tend to label the object and not to grasp the rule of the game. If this is the case, prompt them with questions such as, 'What colour is it?', 'Is it for your hair?' and so on.

Extension
Let older children pass an empty box around and ask them to *imagine* something in it and to describe this to their friends.

LINKS WITH HOME
Ask parents and carers to play a version of this game at home, talking about what is in a parcel or who is outside the window. Explain that the aim is to encourage the child to communicate clearly about something that is not visible to either them or the carers.

LEARNING OBJECTIVE FOR ALL THE CHILDREN
● to link letters to sounds.

INDIVIDUAL LEARNING TARGET
● to join in a large group with increasing confidence.

My favourite letter

Group size
Four to six children.

What you need
A range of toys and empty packaging; postcards with individual letters on.

What to do
Ask the children to sit down together and show them some of the toys and packaging that you have collected. Invite each child to try to find letters and words on the various boxes and help them to read some of the ones that they have spotted.

Next, send the children off around the room to find as many letters and words as they can. Challenge them to find some tiny words and also the biggest words they can.

Sit back down again together and talk about how letters have sounds. Encourage the children to identify what sounds their names begin with. Spread the postcard letters out on the floor and look for the sound that begins each child's name. Now chant or sing the following rhyme:

> I have a favourite letter
> My favourite letter is 'b'
> 'b' is the sound in Bethany's name
> Everyone look for 'b'!
>
> *Hannah Mortimer*

Encourage the children to point to the 'b' card. Repeat for other letters and names of the children in the group.

Special support
Some children with autistic difficulties have an ability to spot letters or numbers and they may excel in this activity. Start with just a few cards, then build up as the children become more familiar with the letter sounds.

Extension
Encourage older children to write the letters needed for the song. Give out large sheets of paper for them to spread on the floor, and washable pens to use.

LINKS WITH HOME
Ask parents and carers to teach their children the first letter sounds of their names, saying, for example, 'Stephen begins with "s"' or 'Zahid begins with "z"'.

MATHEMATICAL DEVELOPMENT

Children who have difficulties within the autistic spectrum are often very good at working with puzzles and solving 'non-verbal' problems. Many of the activities in this chapter build on the strong numerical abilities that these children sometimes have.

Puzzle Olympiad

LEARNING OBJECTIVE FOR ALL THE CHILDREN
● to recognize and re-create simple patterns.

INDIVIDUAL LEARNING TARGET
● to show a particular strength in puzzle-matching.

Group size
All the children at different times.

What you need
A selection of jigsaw puzzles and inset boards (for table-top and floor) at different levels of difficulty.

What to do
You might decide to make this activity a fund-raising event for your group. Plan for a sponsored 'Puzzle Olympiad' well ahead, drawing up sponsor forms and giving these out to families and friends of the group. To remove the competitive aspect, ask for sponsorship for the number of puzzles completed by the group

as a whole and not by individual children. Talk to the children beforehand and discuss what you are raising money for and why.

Spread the puzzles out and invite the children to come to the puzzle area and complete one or more puzzles during the session. Ask one helper to keep a tally count of each puzzle completed.

LINKS WITH HOME
If you borrow puzzles from home, make sure that each child's initials are on the back of each piece of their puzzle. Talk to the parents or carers of any child that you are targeting so that you can make sure that you borrow all their favourite puzzles for your event.

Special support
If necessary, help the children by pointing to pieces to be fitted in next. Draw their attention to any particular skill that the child that you are targeting is showing. Try to engage that child in helping other children who find the puzzles more difficult. Stay close so that the child that you are targeting does this socially and helpfully.

Extension
You might find that the child that you are targeting can complete very complex puzzles. Make sure that they have a clear table to work at if they wish to do a larger puzzle. Praise the children frequently for the way in which they are helping your sponsored event.

LEARNING OBJECTIVE FOR ALL THE CHILDREN
● to recognize numerals 1 to 9.

INDIVIDUAL LEARNING TARGET
● to identify and match numbers 1 to 9.

Match the numbers!

Group size
Two children at a time.

What you need
The photocopiable sheet on page 89; set of plastic numerals 1 to 9 (or draw some on cards); box; colouring crayons or pens.

What to do
Help the child that you are targeting to find a partner to work with, and stay with them. Sit down together at a table. Give the child that you are targeting a copy of the photocopiable sheet and talk about the numbers on it. Place all the plastic numbers in a box and give it to the partner. Support the children as one pulls out a number and names it, passing it to the other child. Encourage the other child to match that number to the corresponding one on the sheet. Continue until all the numbers are placed in their correct positions. Now encourage the children to swap roles and repeat the task.

Special support
The child that you are targeting may already be 'reading' numbers and may be very interested in them. The aim then becomes one of making this number interest into a more social occasion, taking turns with a partner. If the child is still learning early numbers, make a much simpler sheet with the numbers 1 to 3 and with sets of dots to count against each numeral.

Extension
Older children will be able to play this game in groups, more like a 'Bingo' game. As a number is called, they could colour in that number on the sheet of paper. Of course, as all the children have the same sheet of paper, they will win together!

LINKS WITH HOME
If there is a number puzzle that the child that you are targeting particularly enjoys at home, ask the parents or carers to send this in so that their child can show it off to the other children in the group.

LEARNING OBJECTIVE FOR ALL THE CHILDREN
● to use language such as 'more' or 'less'.

INDIVIDUAL LEARNING TARGET
● to develop reciprocal play.

Rice tray

Group size
Four children at a time.

What you need
A sand tray or large plastic bowl; dry rice grains; pouring and filling toys; small plastic animals.

What to do
This is an ideal activity to celebrate Chinese New Year. Fill your usual sand tray or a large bowl with rice grains. Provide scoops, pouring toys and containers for the children to dig and pour with. Stay close as they explore the new materials. Encourage them to pour the rice grains gently over each other's hands. What does it feel like? Encourage them to fill the containers, then ask questions such as, 'Who has more?' and 'Who has less?'. Encourage the children to pour the rice from one container into another. Who has more now? Who has less? Hide small objects such as plastic animals underneath the rice. Encourage the children to feel for them. Who has found more? Who has the most? Count them together to find out. Encourage the children to take turns to hide the animals, then seek them out.

Special support
Encourage the child that you are targeting to take turns with one other child, pouring rice over each other's hands, or filling then emptying a container. Praise them for 'playing with *(child's name)*'. Your aim is to encourage 'reciprocal' play ('my turn, your turn').

Extension
Older children will enjoy measuring and weighing the rice. Provide scales, plastic measuring cylinders and weights. How many ways can they think of for finding out who has more and who has less?

LINKS WITH HOME
Follow up your 'rice' theme with suggestions for meals at home or by sending home rice crackers or fortune cookies.

LEARNING OBJECTIVE FOR ALL THE CHILDREN
● to say and use number names in familiar contexts.

INDIVIDUAL LEARNING TARGET
● to sequence numerals.

Clock-face

Group size
Three or four children at a time.

What you need
The photocopiable sheet on page 90; thin card; crayons or felt-tipped pens; brass split-pin fasteners; scissors; plastic A4 wallets.

What to do
Make two copies of the photocopiable sheet on to thin card for each child. Sit with the children at a table. Look at the clock-face on one of the sheets together and see if the children recognize any of the numbers. Ask questions such as, 'Who is four years old?', then encourage them to point to each number around the clock-face in turn as you count together one to 12. If necessary, say each number for them to copy.

Support the children as they colour in the clock-faces on their first sheets. Help each child to cut around the clock and the clock hand. Use the split-pin fasteners to pin the clock hand to the centre of the clock-face so that it can be rotated. Now help each child to colour in and cut out just the number squares at the bottom of their second sheet.

Let the children have fun as they try matching the number squares to their places on the clock-face. Give each child a plastic wallet to keep all the parts in.

LINKS WITH HOME
Ask parents and carers to play this number matching game with their children at home. Invite them to say the number as their child places each square in place.

Special support
Younger children might need larger pieces to handle; if so, make A3 copies of the photocopiable sheet for them.

Extension
Older children can begin to tell the time by turning the large hand to different numbers and saying what time ('o-clock') it is now.

MATHEMATICAL DEVELOPMENT • MATHEMATICAL DEVELOPMENT • MATHEMATICAL DEVELOPMENT

LEARNING OBJECTIVE FOR ALL THE CHILDREN
● to use everyday words to describe position.

INDIVIDUAL LEARNING TARGET
● to respond to 'under'.

Under or over?

Group size
Two children at a time.

What you need
A 'lift-the-flap' book such as *Where's Spot?* by Eric Hill (Puffin Books); paper; scissors; glue; felt-tipped pen; stapler (adult use).

What to do
Prepare by cutting and folding some of the sheets of paper into a simple eight-page book. Staple the centres together.

Take the children to the book corner and read through your chosen lift-the-flap book together. Read it through once more and encourage one child to lift each flap while you ask the other child, 'Is Spot under the rug?' and so on. Use the story to reinforce the word 'under' as you discover Spot's friends hiding in many different places. Encourage the two children to take turns to lift the flaps or answer your questions. Keep the session relaxed and enjoyable.

Now move to a table and suggest that you make your own 'lift-the-flap' book. Negotiate with the two children who their book will be about, for example, a character called 'Fido'. Draw a title page and write a title such as 'Where's Fido?'. Now support the children as you draw, cut out and stick in a number of pictures of Fido under different objects and pieces of furniture. Help the children to place the flaps carefully and glue them along a hinged edge.

Special support
Give children with language difficulties a choice, for example, 'Is Fido under the rug or under the chair?'.

Extension
Encourage older children to add their own writing to the book.

LINKS WITH HOME
Send the finished book home and ask the parents or carers to read it to their child. Invite the parents or carers of one child to pass it to the parents or carers of the other child when they are ready – this might encourage friendship and conversation.

LEARNING OBJECTIVE FOR ALL THE CHILDREN
● to recognize numerals 1 to 9.

INDIVIDUAL LEARNING TARGET
● to identify numbers on everyday notices and packaging.

Number-spotting

Group size
Four to six children.

What you need
Your usual early years activities and resources; flipchart (or large sheet of paper); pen; additional clocks and calendars; packaging.

What to do
Prepare for this activity, where the children will be searching for numbers in your setting, by displaying the additional packaging, calendars and clocks where the children will be able to find them.

Gather the children around and write a large number (from 1 to 9) on the flipchart. Do any of the children know what this number is? Now invite the children to go on a hunt and to call you when they have found a matching number. Can each child find an example of the number? Support the children as they hunt and find, referring back to the number that you have drawn to compare the two numbers and see if they are the same. Continue with other numbers.

Give the children a general challenge. Where can they see numbers? Explore the packaging and your wall posters to see if anyone can see any more numbers.

Special support
Sometimes children with autistic difficulties have a particular strength and interest in finding and naming numbers. Make this more of a social situation by drawing the other children's attention to what the child that you are targeting has found. In this way, you are drawing the child with difficulties into the learning and play of the other children, therefore including them.

Extension
Older children may be able to read bigger numbers and can be encouraged to show you the largest number that they can see.

LINKS WITH HOME
Talk to the parents or carers of any child that you are targeting to see whether their child has any particular strengths and interests that you can build on in the group.

One, two, three, go!

Group size
Six to ten children.

What you need
An outdoor or indoor play area with your usual equipment and resources.

What to do
This game is based on listening, waiting and action. It can be very difficult for a child with communication difficulties to understand that they must wait for your word before doing something. The game provides an opportunity to support the child in doing this within an enjoyable activity.

Make up an imaginative game in which you all become a team of workers. You might be penguins on parade, the seven dwarfs or a line of soldiers. Encourage all your 'penguins' to stand in line. Is everyone looking? Is everyone listening? Now set the children a simple challenge,

for example, 'When I say "Go!" I want you all to walk to Mrs Singh' or 'When I say "Go!" I want you all to fetch me a red crayon' (or whatever you select). Keep your instructions simple and emphasize key words so that each child can understand. Then say, 'One, two, three, go!'. Call your penguins back, saying, for example, 'Penguins! Attention!', and praise them for listening well, then repeat with a new challenge.

Finish with a penguin waddle around the room or yard: flap your wings as you walk and waggle your tail feathers!

Special support
Gently hold on to the hand of any child who is very impulsive. Use eye contact and a gentle touch to make sure that they are listening to your instructions.

Extension
Encourage older children to help you to think of challenges to make this game fun.

LEARNING OBJECTIVE FOR ALL THE CHILDREN
● to say and use number names in order in familiar contexts.

INDIVIDUAL LEARNING TARGET
● to join in and respond to 'Go!'.

LINKS WITH HOME
Share with parents and carers the approaches that you are using to make sure a child is listening to your instructions. Suggest that they speak the child's name and use eye contact and a gentle touch. They should then check to make sure their child has understood before sending them on their way with a 'One, two, three, go!'.

MATHEMATICAL DEVELOPMENT · MATHEMATICAL DEVELOPMENT · MATHEMATICAL DEVELOPMENT

LEARNING OBJECTIVES FOR ALL THE CHILDREN
● to count three fingers
● to say and use numbers 1 to 3 in a familiar context.

INDIVIDUAL LEARNING TARGET
● to anticipate and respond with humour.

LINKS WITH HOME
Send home song sheets with any songs that the children have particularly responded to.

Three green jellyfish

Group size
Six to ten children.

What you need
A beanie jellyfish or a picture of a jellyfish.

What to do
Sit together in a circle and tell the children that you are going to sing a song about jellyfish. Does anyone know what a jellyfish looks like? Introduce your soft-toy jellyfish or your picture.

Now teach the children the song below. Pause between verses to hold up and count the correct number of fingers, starting with three. Encourage the children to wobble all over when they say, 'jellyfish'. The song can be sung to the tune of 'Three Blind Mice' (Traditional).

> Three green jellyfish, three green jellyfish
> Sat upon a rock, sat upon a rock.
> The first one felt like a swim, you know,
> And slithered away to the sea, you know,
> And left the rest on their own-i-o,
> Just two green jellyfish.

Raise your hands in the air and wobble them down all the way to 'the sea' for the slithering. Repeat one more time until there is one jellyfish left on the rock.

Say, 'Oh dear! The jellyfish was ever so lonely all by itself. What do you do if you are feeling lonely?'. Pause to talk about finding your friends. Then whisper a final verse together.

> One green jellyfish, one green jellyfish
> Sat upon a rock, sat upon a rock.
> It really felt like a swim, you know,
> And slithered away to the sea, you know,
> And left the rock on its own-i-o,
> No green jellyfish.
>
> *Hannah Mortimer*

Special support
You are aiming for the child that you are targeting to join in at whatever level they are capable of. Perhaps they will giggle and anticipate the wobble, or they may accept you wobbling them, or they might watch the other children and copy the actions, though a little late. Make this activity really fun and do not be afraid to have a good laugh together.

Extension
Make three green jellyfish stick puppets with tissue streamers and let the children use them as props for this song.

LEARNING OBJECTIVES FOR ALL THE CHILDREN
● to count reliably
● to find one more or one less than a given number.

INDIVIDUAL LEARNING TARGET
● to look at, remember and identify a set of one, two or three items.

LINKS WITH HOME
Ask parents and carers to encourage their children to count out the knives and forks for supper, or the biscuits on to a plate.

Number nests

Group size
Three children at a time.

What you need
Three plastic beakers (not see-through); box of small cubes or plastic objects (such as cars or counters); three coasters or circular mats.

What to do
Sit together at a table and place the three coasters in a row. Invite one of the children to place one counter on the first coaster. Invite the next child to place two on the second coaster, and another to place three counters on the third one. Count out aloud together as the counters are placed. Now tell the children that you are going to play a trick.

Cover each set of counters with one of the beakers. Invite one child to lift the beaker that has one counter underneath, another to find the set of two counters and a third child to find the set of three. Praise the children for remembering where the counters are. Next time, muddle the beakers up so that each child has to lift and search for the right number.

Invite the children to take it in turns to mix the beakers up and ask the next child to 'find one' (or two or three). This activity encourages children to make quick judgements based on the appearance of the set. You can check their judgement by counting out the number, but it should soon be possible for the children to recognize 'one-ness', 'two-ness' and 'three-ness'.

Special support
Children with autistic difficulties may quickly learn to 'read' written numbers, but will sometimes have more difficulty in counting out objects, especially in a social game. This activity should help them to develop counting skills and also to use their number knowledge more socially, communicating it to other children.

Extension
With older children, use five or six counters. Start by arranging them as for the dots on a dice. Later, try with a random arrangement of counters on each coaster.

LEARNING OBJECTIVE FOR ALL THE CHILDREN
● to count reliably up to 20.

INDIVIDUAL LEARNING TARGET
● to tolerate physical contact.

LINKS WITH HOME
Ask the parents or carers of the child that you are targeting to spend time playing 'Chase and catch' with their child to provide an enjoyable way for them to cope with physical contact.

Counting heads

Group size
Eight to 20 children.

What you need
A large floor space.

What to do
Sit together in a circle and introduce the song below, which can be sung to the tune of 'Twinkle, Twinkle, Little Star' (Traditional):

> Two little rabbits came to play
> On a sunny holiday.
> They had such fun as you can see,
> They even had a splendid tea!
> Two little rabbits came to play
> Who will join them, who can say?
>
> *Hannah Mortimer*

Start by inviting one of the children to join you in the middle of the circle – for example, the child that you are targeting. Touch your own head and theirs gently together, inviting all the children to count with you, 'One, two'. Hold the child's hands as you dance around singing the song. In the third and fourth lines, make sure that you mime having a party! At the end of the verse, turn to the children and ask if there are any more rabbits who would like to play. Stop to touch the heads of the rabbits in the centre of the circle as you count again, asking all the children to count with you. Substitute the new number of rabbits into line one. Build up the number over four or five verses, until you are all partying in the middle!

Special support
Some children with autistic difficulties try to avoid physical contact. Keep this game fun and non-threatening so that they feel relaxed when you touch their heads gently.

Extension
Invite older children to lead the counting, asking them, 'How many rabbits have come to play now?'.

KNOWLEDGE AND UNDERSTANDING OF THE WORLD

For children with autistic difficulties, the world can sometimes seem unpredictable. These activities will help them to develop an understanding of the objects, people and places that they see.

What next?

Group size
Four to six children.

What you need
A felt board and Velcro tabs, or a whiteboard and Blu-Tack; sheets of A5 paper; felt-tipped pens.

What to do
Sit down with the children and talk about their typical session. Ask them to tell you all the things that they do in your group. Take one idea at a time and draw a simple representation of this on to a sheet of paper, for example, a water tray, a paint pot or a teddy in a bed. Spread the sheets out in front of you. Have you missed anything out? Make sure that you have a picture for any 'link' times such as group time, snack time and saying 'goodbye'.

Now use the Blu-Tack or Velcro tabs to arrange a few of these pictures in a sequence on a felt board or whiteboard to make a visual timetable for the children. Encourage them to refer to the timetable from time to time between activities, and use it as a springboard to talk about the past, the present and the future, asking questions such as, 'What did you do before story time?', 'What will you do next?' and so on.

Special support
Work individually to create a very simple representation of the child's session (see illustration below). Some children will find a left-to-right sequence easier, while others will prefer a top-to-bottom sequence. Use it to help the child to understand what will happen next.

Extension
Look at other simple timetables and talk about different ways in which we record the day, for example, school timetables, lists, diaries and calendars.

LEARNING OBJECTIVES FOR ALL THE CHILDREN
● to investigate objects and materials
● to complete a task.

INDIVIDUAL LEARNING TARGET
● to finish one activity in order to move on to the next.

I've finished!

Group size
One child at a time.

What you need
A selection of simple puzzles and formboards; shallow box.

What to do
In some ways, this activity contradicts early years philosophy of 'learning through play'. Usually, you are striving to extend children's thinking and learning so that they think flexibly and enjoy the process of what they are doing rather than the end product, developing creativity and thoughtfulness. This is why it is aimed at just one or two children who may have autistic difficulties or short attention spans.

Set up the puzzles in a pile to the left of the child. Support them as they work through each one, using finger-pointing or hand-over-hand support to help them to place the pieces correctly. When the puzzle is completed, engage the child's eye contact and make a clear sign for 'finished'. Clap hands and celebrate. Then encourage the child to place the puzzle in a 'finished' box to their right. Work through several puzzles while the child is still enjoying success.

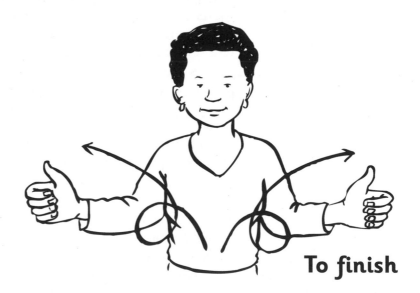

To finish

Special support
This is a variation on the TEACCH approach (see page 21), which uses clear visual signals to help children to see what is expected of them. This approach can be used to show a child how much work they should do, what work they should do, when they have finished and what happens next (these are concepts that children with autistic difficulties find hard to grasp).

Extension
Use the 'finished' box throughout the session for completed drawings or models. Use the sign for 'finished' between different activities on your visual timetable, too (see the activity 'What next?' on page 55).

LINKS WITH HOME
Suggest that parents and carers use the 'finished' sign at home, too. It can be used at the end of routine tasks such as getting dressed or eating.

LEARNING OBJECTIVE FOR ALL THE CHILDREN
● to observe and find out about features in the place they live.

INDIVIDUAL LEARNING TARGETS
● to feel motivated to persist in an activity
● to play appropriately with tracks and trains.

Train tracks

Group size
Two or three children at a time.

What you need
A train set with interlocking track, engines and buildings; clear floor space; card; pen.

What to do
Place just a few sections of track down and the rest of the train set near by. Put up a card making it clear how many children can play in the area at once, perhaps showing a symbol of three children. When the children have started to play and to develop the game, stay close to help them to think about what they are doing and extend their ideas. Ask questions such as, 'Isn't the bridge high – how will you get the track up there?', 'Where are the people going?', 'What is the goods train carrying?' and so on. Provide just enough ideas to spark their imagination. If necessary, step in to help them to negotiate sharing and turn-taking.

Special support
Activities based on train tracks are often a source of intense interest for children who have autistic difficulties. Your task is to help them to see the game more flexibly, socially and imaginatively. At first, it will simply be a matter of helping them to tolerate your presence as you add a carriage or pass the next piece of track. Later, encourage the child to stay calm when a second child is playing with a similar track beside them. Finally, help them to see the game imaginatively and to play with the second child.

Extension
Set the children a challenge to work out. Place two toy buildings about a metre apart. Can the children find a way to join the track so that it will go from one building to the other?

LINKS WITH HOME
Ask the parents or carers of a new child to tell you about their child's favourite games and play things at home, so that you can build on this interest through your activities in the group.

Garage game

Group size
Three or four children at once.

What you need
Your usual wheeled bikes and cars; outdoor play area; large cardboard boxes; sharp scissors (adult use); selection of car tools such as spanners, wrenches, nuts and bolts.

What to do
Sit down together with the children and invite them to tell you if they have any ideas for a garage game. Ask if anyone has been to a garage. What was wrong with the car? How did they fix it? What tools did they use? Build on the children's interest and show them the tools that you have collected. Use the children's ideas to convert cardboard boxes into a garage (by cutting an opening in the front of a large box) and tool boxes (by lifting the flaps of a narrow box). You can make tall boxes into petrol pumps. Set up the garage together and encourage the children as they pretend to be mechanics and drivers. Support them as they continue to enjoy the role-play.

Special support
If the child that you are targeting is particularly fascinated by wheels, they will enjoy staying in the garage and playing with the wheels. Your role is to make the play more appropriate and to prevent the child from becoming too absorbed in themselves, simply by being there and talking gently to them about what they are doing.

Extension
Let older children design miniature garages and tools for the small cars out of smaller boxes and card.

LEARNING OBJECTIVE FOR ALL THE CHILDREN
● to identify the uses of everyday technology.

INDIVIDUAL LEARNING TARGET
● to identify wheels.

LINKS WITH HOME
Some children insist on bringing in certain cars from home and holding on to them throughout the session. Provide a special 'garage' to park the cars on as they arrive in your setting.

Wheels

Group size
Four to six children at a time.

What you need
Your usual selection of indoor and outdoor toys and play things; hard and rough floor surfaces and inclines for rolling the toys on; picture book about wheels, such as *Wheels* by Shirley Hughes (Walker Books).

What to do
For this activity about finding and collecting wheeled vehicles and toys, and about exploring how they work, start by looking through a picture book together. Notice all the wheels shown and talk about the jobs that they do in helping things to move, work or travel.

Now challenge the children to go on a 'wheel hunt'. Ask them to look around the room and to fetch you something with four wheels on. Can they find something with two wheels? And with three wheels? Now stop to compare the sizes of the wheels and ask questions such as, 'Who can find a very big wheel?' and 'What is the smallest wheel that you can find?'.

Collect together some of the wheeled vehicles that you have found and work out the best way to help the wheels to move. Do they travel better on the rough carpet or the smooth floor? Do they roll uphill as well as downhill? Can you make a slide for them to roll without tumbling off?

Special support
Some children with autistic difficulties can become very absorbed in watching wheels turn or collecting wheeled vehicles. This activity provides a way of harnessing their intense interest and making it more socially appropriate.

Extension
Let older children use Lego Meccano to work out how gear wheels operate together.

LEARNING OBJECTIVE FOR ALL THE CHILDREN
● to select the tools and techniques needed to make a sandwich.

INDIVIDUAL LEARNING TARGET
● to follow a sequence of actions.

Sandwich sequence

Group size
Four to six children at a time.

What you need
The photocopiable sheet on page 91; slices of bread; spread; slices of cheese, tomato and ham; lettuce; bread boards; plates; sharp knife (adult use); knives to spread with.

What to do
Make several photocopies of the photocopiable and cut one of them up into four sections.

Gather the children together, sitting around a table or on the floor. Show them the picture sequence from the photocopiable sheet. Talk about making a sandwich and each stage that is involved. Now place the four pieces of paper on the floor or table and challenge different children to place the sequence in the correct order. Talk about what happens first, then and last.

Check for any food allergies and dietary requirements, then suggest that the children make their own sandwiches. Place the picture sequence in front of them and support them as they work out what to do first. Let them choose which fillings to layer inside their sandwiches. Use a sharp knife to cut each sandwich into four when the process is complete. Lift the sandwich on to the child's plate and save the sandwiches for snack time. Make it a sociable occasion as you sit together and talk about your fillings and the different tastes.

Special support
Picture sequences are a useful way of helping children with autistic difficulties to understand what comes next and what to do once they have finished something. Use a felt board and Velcro patches to make visual timetables (see the activity 'What next?' on page 55).

Extension
Invent new, exciting and multicultural sandwich fillings and arrange a tasting session. Vote on the group's favourite sandwich filling!

LINKS WITH HOME
Give each child a copy of the photocopiable sheet and ask parents and carers to support the children in making their own sandwiches.

LEARNING OBJECTIVE FOR ALL THE CHILDREN
● to identify body parts.

INDIVIDUAL LEARNING TARGETS
● to develop confidence in physical contact
● to develop body awareness.

My turn, your turn

Group size
An even number of children up to eight.

What you need
Just the children.

What to do
Help the children to choose a partner and to sit down on the floor opposite each other. Teach them the song below, which can be sung to the tune of 'The Hokey Cokey' (Traditional):

> You touch your nose right here, your nose right here,
> My nose, your nose, touch your nose again,
> You squeeze your nose together with a one, two, three;
> That's what it's all about!

Emphasize the different body parts as you encourage the children to gently touch their own noses and their partners' in the second line of the song. Then sing the chorus to 'The Hokey Cokey' while clapping, and make up new verses, for example:

> You touch your ear right here, your ear right here,
> My ear, your ear, touch your ear again,
> You wiggle your ears around with a one, two, three;
> That's what it's all about!
>
> *Hannah Mortimer*

Encourage the children to help you to make up new verses. Keep the pace slow and praise them for being gentle with each other.

Special support
Start by sitting down with the child that you are targeting and a large teddy bear. Guide their hands gently as you sing, 'My nose, your nose' to the teddy bear. Once the child feels comfortable with this, help them to point to their own nose and then yours.

LINKS WITH HOME
Ask parents and carers to help their children to point to different parts of their bodies in a mirror at home.

Extension
Challenge the children to think of more action rhymes that mention body parts, for example, 'Heads and Shoulders, Knees and Toes' (Traditional).

LEARNING OBJECTIVE FOR ALL THE CHILDREN
● to identify some features of events they observe.

INDIVIDUAL LEARNING TARGET
● to join in simple actions in a group.

LINKS WITH HOME
Suggest that parents and carers enjoy this action rhyme on the way home with their children. Encourage them to help their children to make up new verses to suit their method of travel to and from your setting.

Wheels on the bus

Group size
Eight to 24 children.

What you need
Several sheets of card; thick felt-tipped pens; floor space.

What to do
On each card, draw one picture to represent the items mentioned in the song 'The Wheels on the Bus' (Traditional). Include a wheel, set of windscreen wipers, horn in a steering wheel, bell button, baby, Mum and Grandpa. Have blank cards ready to add other pictures to represent other verses that you might sing.

Ask the children to sit in a circle on the floor. Place all the cards except the 'wheel' on to the floor in the centre of the circle. Hold up the 'wheel' card as you start to sing 'The wheels on the bus go round and round'. Make the action as you sing the words.

Invite a child to turn over another card and to sing a second verse based on the new picture. Continue until you have uncovered all the cards and sung several verses.

Now take some blank cards and ask the children what else they have noticed on bus journeys. Draw new pictures for the 'driver', the 'conductor', the 'shopping' and so on. Make up new actions and verses to go with these.

Special support
Some children with autistic difficulties find it very hard to communicate in words. They might be able to use the action for 'The wheels on the bus go round and round' to make you understand that they would like to sing. You can also show them the picture cards to encourage them to carry out the right actions for each verse.

Extension
Older children will enjoy helping to make picture cards and to invent new verses.

LEARNING OBJECTIVE FOR ALL THE CHILDREN
- to look closely at differences and change.

INDIVIDUAL LEARNING TARGET
- to share and understand humour.

That's very odd!

Group size
Four children.

What you need
An enlarged copy of the photocopiable sheet on page 92; card; glue; scissors.

What to do
Cut the enlarged photocopiable sheet into four pictures and use glue to mount these on to sheets of card. You could invite an older child to colour the pictures at this stage.

Explain to the children that there is something wrong with each picture. Can they see what it is? Give each child one of the picture cards and invite them to look at it carefully, but not to tell the others what is wrong! This will take support as once the children identify what is wrong they will be keen to speak! Use gesture and comments to help them, saying, for example, 'Have you noticed? Well done!'.

Swap the pictures around until each child has seen all four. Now look at them as a group, talking about each picture in turn. Encourage the children to identify something very odd and funny. The pictures will provide useful talking points for you to discuss familiar situations and to share humour with the children.

Special support
Children with autistic difficulties often find it hard to see humour because they take things very literally. Double meanings are especially hard for them. However, visual humour is often the first kind of joking to emerge. Share with the child that you are targeting a game about funny hats and noses so that you can introduce the words 'That's funny!'. Show the child in a concrete way why the pictures represent an unlikely situation, for example, trying putting on some jeans over your head!

Extension
Ask older children to think of other funny situations that you could draw together.

LINKS WITH HOME
Teach the children a simple 'double-meaning joke' to share with their parents and carers at home – for example, 'What did the policeman say to his chest? You're under a vest!'.

LEARNING OBJECTIVE FOR ALL THE CHILDREN
● to find out about their school environment.

INDIVIDUAL LEARNING TARGET
● to feel confident when starting at a new school.

Moving on

Group size
Whole group.

What you need
A visit to the children's next school or class; camera; adult helpers (one to every three or four children).

What to do
Arrange a visit to the children's receiving school or their next class in school well ahead of the time that they are due to start there. Consider the visit through the children's eyes. What are the first things that they will notice? What might they be anxious about?

Keep the visit simple so that the children do not have to take in too much information at once. Make sure that they do something specific when they get there, such as play in the Reception class or visit the outdoor play area. Lend the camera to the children so that they can take pictures of what they liked at school, in order to mount these into a book entitled 'Starting school'. Make sure that you visit the coat area, the dining area and the toilets, too. Talk in concrete terms about what will happen when the children start school and point out all the interesting things going on there. Sometimes it is worth telling them things that seem obvious to adults, for example, that they do not need to be able to read yet as they will learn how to at school!

Special support
Make sure that there are activities or play equipment that will have a high personal meaning for the child with autistic difficulties. Help them to start playing straight away. Use the time to find out what the daily routines are so that you can build photographs into a visual timetable.

Extension
Encourage older children to dictate to you or write down their impressions, which you can add to your book.

LINKS WITH HOME
If possible, arrange for parents and carers to join you for the visit so that they can look around the school with their children.

PHYSICAL DEVELOPMENT

The activities in this chapter encourage children's movement, balance and physical skills. Children with autistic difficulties often enjoy physical play so these ideas will provide good opportunities for them to develop their physical skills.

Taxi!

LEARNING OBJECTIVE FOR ALL THE CHILDREN
● to show awareness of space, of themselves and of others.

INDIVIDUAL LEARNING TARGET
● to play co-operatively with another child.

Group size
Four to six children.

What you need
Large push-along toys; 'Taxi' sign; open space.

What to do
This activity works well for children at the earliest stages of co-operative play. You will need to supervise them carefully to make sure that they all stay safe.

Get out your large push-along toys. This activity can run alongside the children's usual outdoor playtime, when all your other wheeled toys are in use as well. Gather a few children together and suggest that you play a game of 'Taxi!'. Encourage two or three of the children to be the 'taxi driver', pushing along a wheeled toy each. Stand with the other children next to the 'Taxi' sign and 'hail' one of the 'taxis' by calling out 'Taxi!'. Help the children to negotiate where they want to go and to say 'please' and 'thank you'. Send them off in pairs on their taxi journeys, with the 'drivers' pushing the 'customers' carefully on the wheeled toys. Swap places after a while, so that the drivers become customers. When the children are playing independently, stand back and let them develop the game.

Special support
This activity encourages children to play alongside one another. The child with autistic and communication difficulties that you are targeting will be happy to be driven around, and the other children will enjoy including them in their game.

Extension
Build this into a more complex game by imagining a shopping trip or a car journey.

LINKS WITH HOME
Ask parents and carers to supervise as their children play together helpfully at the playground. Perhaps one could gently push another on the swing, or two could take turns on the slide.

PHYSICAL DEVELOPMENT · PHYSICAL DEVELOPMENT · PHYSICAL DEVELOPMENT

LEARNING OBJECTIVE FOR ALL THE CHILDREN
● to use a range of small and large equipment.

INDIVIDUAL LEARNING TARGET
● to give and to roll a ball to another child.

Ball swap

Group size
Eight to 12 children.

What you need
A large basketball; open space.

What to do
Children and adults will find if helpful to wear trousers or PE shorts to carry out this activity. Start by sitting down together in a large circle. Achieve this to music by joining hands and walking around chanting, 'We can make a circle, we can make a circle!'. As you walk around, slowly make the circle bigger until the children are evenly spaced out. Then ask the children to drop hands and sit down. Invite them to sit with their legs out in front of them in a V-shape. Pick up the ball and join the circle yourself.

Now teach the children the song below, which can be sung to the tune of 'Row, Row, Row Your Boat' (Traditional):

> Roll, roll, roll the ball
> Right across the room.
> Roll the ball to *(child's name)*
> Who'll catch it if *(she)* can!
>
> *Hannah Mortimer*

Sing the song through once, adding the name of one of the children opposite you to the third line. Now push and roll the ball across the circle to that child. If your aim goes astray, then whoever catches it should pass it from child to child all the way to the child that you named. Encourage that child to think of someone to roll the ball to, helping them with names if necessary. Repeat until everyone who wants to has had a turn catching and returning.

Special support
Start with just two of you with your legs in a V-shape to funnel the ball. Play a rolling game in order to teach reciprocity ('my turn, your turn'). Then start to include two or three other children.

Extension
Let older children bounce or throw the ball to one another, too.

LINKS WITH HOME
Ask parents and carers to help their children to develop rolling and aiming skills by playing a rolling game with a football at home.

LEARNING OBJECTIVE FOR ALL THE CHILDREN
● to move with confidence, control and co-ordination.

INDIVIDUAL LEARNING TARGET
● to respond to a signal for 'stop'.

Tambourine shake

Group size
Whole group.

What you need
A large tambourine.

What to do
This activity will encourage the whole group to concentrate as a unit. Ask the children to stand in a circle and tell them that you are going to play some shaking music. Explain that when they hear it, they have to shake all over: shake their arms, their toes and their bodies all over. When the music stops, they should stop, too. Check that they are listening and looking.

Move around the circle as you shake the tambourine loudly, encouraging the children to shake their bodies. Then beat the tambourine once loudly, stopping absolutely still. Praise the children by name for looking and listening. Repeat three or four times, encouraging laughter and giggles as you shake, and scanning all the children's faces when you have stopped. Keep the activity fun and challenging. Pretend to put the tambourine away, but then let it shake just one last time. Praise all the children for looking and listening so well.

Now move into a large space and encourage the children to move when they hear the tambourine and stop absolutely still when it stops. Praise them for holding their positions and staying still.

Special support
Try to catch the attention of the child that you are targeting. You might be able to include them by giving them the tambourine to shake or bang while the other children move.

Extension
Listen to several musical instruments together and ask the children to invent a way of moving to go with each one.

LINKS WITH HOME
Ask parents and carers to help their children to find different ways of making sounds at home with pots, pans, jars of rice and so on.

LEARNING OBJECTIVE FOR ALL THE CHILDREN
● to balance with control and co-ordination.

INDIVIDUAL LEARNING TARGET
● to tolerate playing with a partner.

LINKS WITH HOME
Ask parents and carers to challenge their children with balancing games at home. Can they walk on their toes? Can they stand on one leg and count to five? Can they walk on their heels, on the insides of their feet, or on the outsides of their feet? Can they jump with two feet together?

Rocking song

Group size
Even numbers of children up to 12.

What you need
A carpeted floor.

What to do
Help the children to each choose a partner and invite them to sit facing each other on the floor. Start with a familiar rocking song such as 'Row, Row, Row Your Boat' (see the activity 'Longboat' on page 71). Help the children to rock backwards and forwards very slowly as they sing, without losing their balance. Then challenge them to sing the same song, but with a slow sideways movement, leaning to one side, then to the other. Can they still keep their balance without falling? (Give plenty of attention to children who manage to keep their balance, rather than to the ones who fall over in laughter!)

Now show the children how they can sit back to back with their elbows entwined and rock backwards and forwards by moving together carefully. Again, praise the children who work together.

Finally, try side-to-side rocking with backs together.

Special support
Start by working with the child that you are targeting yourself. The first stage will be to rock together, both of you facing the same way and the child in front of you. In this way, a child who dislikes eye contact can still feel relaxed. Gradually work up to the other stages, sitting behind the child to support them and including a second child as a partner.

Extension
With older children, make up silly versions for the last two lines, for example, 'If you see a hippopotamus, don't forget to make-a-lot-o-fuss!'.

Heads and shoulders

Group size
Eight to 24 children.

What you need
An open space.

What to do
Teach the children the words of the traditional rhyme 'Heads and Shoulders, Knees and Toes':

> Heads, shoulders, knees and toes, knees and toes, *(twice)*
> Eyes and ears, and mouth and nose,
> Heads, shoulders, knees and toes, knees and toes.

Start very slowly and allow most of the children to join in independently from the start, copying your actions as you point to each body part on yourself. Pair each child who is still learning body parts with an adult or an older child.

The first time through the song, the helper should point to each part mentioned on the child, emphasizing the key words such as 'head'.

The second time through, take it just as slowly, but ask the helpers to encourage (with hand-over-hand support if necessary) the child to point to themselves.

The third time through, take it at a fast pace for fun. Each helper should do the pointing again on to the child, ending with a laugh and a tickle. Meanwhile, the children who are joining in the activity independently will have the challenge of doing so very quickly!

Special support
Children with autistic difficulties may find close physical presence or contact quite threatening. By using rough-and-tumble play and action rhymes, you can help them to feel relaxed about this and make it fun.

Extension
Build in body parts to other familiar action songs, for example, sing, 'If you're happy and you know it, touch your ankle'.

LEARNING OBJECTIVES FOR ALL THE CHILDREN
● to show awareness of their bodies to move with co-ordination.

INDIVIDUAL LEARNING TARGETS
● to accept and enjoy physical contact
● to develop body awareness.

LINKS WITH HOME
Encourage parents and carers to use the correct names for the different parts of the body.

PHYSICAL DEVELOPMENT · PHYSICAL DEVELOPMENT

LEARNING OBJECTIVE FOR ALL THE CHILDREN
● to show awareness of space, of themselves and of others.

INDIVIDUAL LEARNING TARGETS
● to make eye contact when greeted
● to accept close proximity with confidence.

LINKS WITH HOME
If any children have poor looking-and-listening skills, suggest that parents and carers make eye contact with them and say their names before giving them instructions. This will help 'selective deafness'.

The greeting game

Group size
12 to 25 children.

What you need
An open space.

What to do
Sit down together in a large circle, using the musical method described in the activity 'Moving on' on page 66 if this helps. Encourage the children to listen carefully as you chant this request:

> Stand up Marie
> And stand up Josie
> And c-h-a-n-g-e places!

Make a swooping intonation on the word 'change' as you encourage the children to cross the circle and sit down in each other's places. Once the children have become used to this activity, introduce a variation. This time, ask them to look at each other and wave as they pass each other in the centre of the circle. Continue to use your chant each time. As another variation, the children can shake hands or turn each other around as they cross the circle.

Special support
Children with communication and autistic difficulties may find it hard to make eye contact. They need to practise this in relaxed situations. Start by asking them to change places with another adult who can encourage a fleeting eye contact as the two pass each other.

Extension
Invite older children to give the directions and to invent new ways of greeting each other as they cross the circle, for example, bowing or blowing a kiss.

LEARNING OBJECTIVE FOR ALL THE CHILDREN
● to balance with control and co-ordination.

INDIVIDUAL LEARNING TARGETS
● to be aware of their own space
● to tolerate close contact with other children.

Longboat

Group size
Six to 12 children.

What you need
A carpeted floor area.

What to do
Use the traditional rhyme 'Row, Row, Row Your Boat' to practise balancing skills. Ask the children to sit on the floor and sing:

> Row, row, row your boat
> Gently down the stream,
> Merrily, merrily, merrily, merrily,
> Life is but a dream.
> (Traditional)

The first time you sing this, allow the children to rock in their places as if they were rowing a boat. Children sitting on their knees can be rocked gently.

When the children are more familiar with the song, encourage them to join in pairs, facing each other and rocking gently forwards and backwards as they hold hands. Now vary your movements by trying gentle back-to-back rocking.

Finally, place all the children in a long line, sitting on the floor with legs either side of the child in front. Now row your longboat together! You can add variations to the last line, for example, 'If you see a crocodile, don't forget to scream', 'If you see a tall giraffe, don't forget to laugh!'.

Special support
Help children with particular needs by positioning an adult behind them, legs either side of the child. Alternatively, younger children can be sat astride the adult's knee. Always aim to help the children to join in fully with another child, if at all possible.

Extension
Make a longboat out of carton boxes, sit inside and row to the song.

LINKS WITH HOME
Suggest to parents and carers that they use this rhyme with their children at bedtime. It also makes a gentle lullaby when cuddling sad children.

LEARNING OBJECTIVE FOR ALL THE CHILDREN
● to move with imagination.

INDIVIDUAL LEARNING TARGETS
● to give a lead to others
● to recognize when they are being copied
● to copy others.

Pied piper

Group size
Ten to 20 children.

What you need
A big drum; beater; large, open, outdoor or indoor space; adult helper.

What to do
If the children are not familiar with the terms, start by explaining to them what to 'line up' and 'follow' mean. Do this by marching at the front of a line of children, beating your drum and asking the children to march when you march and to stop when you stop. In this way, you can stop as soon as the line disintegrates, or if you are about to be overtaken, and help the children to form the line again!

Now, pass the drum to your helper and ask them to keep a strong beat as you march in front of the line waving your hands. Encourage the children to copy you. Ask the helper to stop after 30 seconds or so. Next, choose a new action, perhaps turning around or crouching low and swinging your arms as you move. Again, encourage the children to copy. Once the children understand the principles of 'Follow-my-leader', encourage different children to take turns to lead as you all copy. Again, it is helpful to stop the beat from time to time before you switch movements.

Special support
Children with autistic difficulties sometimes find looking and copying difficult. Make sure that they are second in line to make copying easier for them. Arrange to hold their hand and support them as they take a turn at leading. Keep their actions simple, for example, just moving and stopping, with everyone else moving and stopping behind them. Point out that the other children are copying them.

Extension
Older children can cope with merging one activity into the next. This involves much greater concentration and imagination.

LINKS WITH HOME
Ask parents and carers to encourage their children to copy them when they are doing routine tasks around the house, such as wiping up dishes, tidying up or dusting.

SPECIAL NEEDS in the early years: Autistic spectrum difficulties

LEARNING OBJECTIVES FOR ALL THE CHILDREN

● to handle tools, objects safely and with increasing control
● to travel under a tunnel.

INDIVIDUAL LEARNING TARGET

● to receive and pass on a small object.

Conveyor belt

Group size
12 to 25 children.

What you need

A plastic tunnel (or large carton boxes); solid chair or low table; toy hammer, chisel, saw and drill; buckets; spade; large wooden bricks; large box.

What to do

Put all the bricks and tools in the large box and place it next to you. Ask the children to sit on the floor in a circle. Teach them this building song, sung to the tune of 'Here We Go Round the Mulberry Bush' (Traditional):

This is the way we build a wall, build a wall, build a wall
This is the way we build a wall, working all together!

Now take one brick at a time out of the box and show the children how to pass it from hand to hand around the circle. When it reaches the last child, ask them to start building a wall with the bricks. Sing the verse again two or three times as you pass bricks around the circle.

Next, ask the children to move aside as you place a tunnel on one side of your circle. You can make one out of carton boxes if you do not have a plastic one. Invite one child to sit in the tunnel. This time, pass buckets and spades around the circle as you sing:

This is the way we dig a tunnel, dig a tunnel, dig a tunnel,
This is the way we dig a tunnel, working all together!

Encourage the children to pass the objects carefully from hand to hand all the way around the circle and via the child in the tunnel.

The last verse requires one of the children to sit safely on the low table or chair as the children pass the carpenter's tools around the circle and up to the 'roofer'.

This is the way we build a roof, build a roof, build a roof,
This is the way we build a roof, working all together!

Special support

Learning to receive a proffered item and to pass it on again can be difficult for a child with autistic difficulties. This activity makes it fun.

Extension

Encourage older children to think about all the building trades involved in constructing a house and the tools that are needed.

LINKS WITH HOME

Ask the parents or carers of the child that you are targeting to play a 'Give and take' game with a ball, saying, for example, 'Harry have it... Daddy have it...'.

LEARNING OBJECTIVE FOR ALL THE CHILDREN
● to use a range of small and large equipment.

INDIVIDUAL LEARNING TARGET
● to join in a group game with confidence.

People skittles

Group size
Four or five children.

What you need
A large inflatable ball; clear floor space; three or four plastic skittles; ball.

What to do
Take the children into a clear space and ask if any of them have played 'Skittles' or 'Bowling' before. Can they describe to you what happens? Show the children the skittles and support them as they work out what to do with them and how to place them. Let each child have a few turns.

Now, encourage the children to take turns at being 'skittles' or being the bowler. Ask one child to roll the ball from a short distance away, while the other children stand still in a cluster. You will have to position everybody, praising them for staying still! As soon as a 'skittle' is touched by the ball, encourage the 'skittle' to shout 'YES!' and to sit down at the side of the space. Invite the bowler to keep trying until all the skittles are 'down'.

Special support
This activity is suitable for a child who finds social contact difficult. You will need to direct them closely when they bowl. An adult helper should stand with the child to hold their hands when they are 'skittles'. Keep the activity short and successful.

Extension
Let older children play with a full set of plastic skittles and a ball, taking turns to knock the skittles over.

LINKS WITH HOME
Consider a group outing to a bowling alley, asking as many parents and carers as possible to join you to help on the day.

CREATIVE DEVELOPMENT

In this chapter, you will find ideas for using music, movement and art to encourage withdrawn children to be more responsive to their surroundings. Let them explore and enjoy sounds, sights and movement with these activities.

LEARNING OBJECTIVE FOR ALL THE CHILDREN
● to express and communicate their ideas using sounds.

INDIVIDUAL LEARNING TARGET
● to look at and copy another child.

Follow the leader

Group size
Whole group.

What you need
A selection of percussion musical instruments such as drums, shakers, bells, scrapers and so on; musical tape or CD; tape recorder or CD player.

What to do

Put the musical instruments in the centre of the circle and invite each child to come and choose one for themselves. If you have more than ten children, ask a few named children at a time to come forwards, in order to avoid everyone choosing at once. Make sure that all the adults have an instrument each, too.

Invite the children to watch you and say, 'When I play, you play too. When I stop, you stop too'. Turn on the music on the tape recorder or CD player. After a minute or so, stop and look around at the children's faces and praise the children by name for looking and listening.

Repeat this three or four times, perhaps 'catching them out' with a very short passage towards the end. Now encourage different children to make a musical sound with their instruments and ask the rest of the group to copy, starting and stopping as the lead child stops and starts.

Special support
This activity is ideal for children who appear to 'be in a world of their own', paying little attention to other adults and children around them. Give the child that you are targeting their favourite instrument. When they start to play it, start the music so that all the children can play as well. When the child happens to stop, stop the music so that all the other children stop too. You may be rewarded with a huge smile as the child suddenly realizes the effect that they are having on all the other children.

Extension
Invite different children to conduct the band using signals for 'start' and 'stop'.

LINKS WITH HOME
Give each child a copy of the photocopiable sheet on page 93 and ask parents and carers to talk about the instruments with their children.

LEARNING OBJECTIVE FOR ALL THE CHILDREN
● to respond in a variety of ways to what they see and hear.

INDIVIDUAL LEARNING TARGETS
● to watch and listen carefully
● to ask or signal for 'more'.

Musical boxes

Group size
Two or three children.

What you need
A selection of clockwork musical boxes; display table; table-cloth; cards; pen; adult helper.

What to do
Arrange an attractive cloth on a display table and place a selection of musical boxes on it. Write cards saying 'What can you hear?' and 'Which do you like best?'. Ask a helper to sit by the table all the time that the children are visiting it.

At the beginning of the session, tell the children about the musical boxes and explain that they have been lent to you. Say that they need to be opened or turned very carefully, and explain to the children that if they do this they will hear a surprise. Ask who would like to go to the table first, and arrange for two or three children at a time to visit it.

Ask the helper to hold the box while a child operates it, and to talk to the children about the sounds that they can hear. Then they should ask the child which of the boxes they prefer and why.

Special support
Some children with autistic difficulties are captivated by the sounds of musical boxes. If the activity proves very popular with them, suggest that they remain with the display to show the musical boxes to the other children. Try to keep this a social occasion, inviting the child that you are targeting to show and share. Encourage them to ask or gesture for 'more'.

Extension
Challenge the children to sing back the tunes that they can hear from the boxes.

LINKS WITH HOME
Write to parents and carers well ahead to ask if they could lend you any musical boxes that are not too delicate or old. Clarify that an adult will look after them at all times.

CREATIVE DEVELOPMENT • CREATIVE DEVELOPMENT • CREATIVE DEVELOPMENT

LEARNING OBJECTIVES FOR ALL THE CHILDREN
● to respond in a variety of ways to what they see
● to use their imagination in art and design.

INDIVIDUAL LEARNING TARGET
● to share and communicate pleasure.

LINKS WITH HOME
Ask parents and carers to help their children to look out for repeating patterns in wallpaper, fabrics, tiles and carpets at home. Suggest that they consider which colours look attractive together.

Kaleidoscopes

Group size
Three or four children at a time.

What you need
A collection of kaleidoscopes; display table; table-cloth; cards; pen; sheets of paper; scissors; coloured shape stickers; adult helper.

What to do
Arrange an attractive cloth on a display table and place a selection of kaleidoscopes on it. Write cards saying 'What can you see?' and 'Which do you like best?' to invite the children to look at and compare the different kaleidoscopes. You will need an adult helper to sit with the kaleidoscopes and to help the children to look through them. Place your display table just near to a bright window or light source, where the children will be able to hold the kaleidoscopes up to the light.

After the children have admired the patterns of the kaleidoscopes, move to the display table and invite them to make kaleidoscope patterns using the paper and stickers. Help them to cut a large round shape out of the paper first, then encourage them to select and stick the shapes on to it, making it as colourful as they can.

Special support
Children with autistic difficulties are sometimes more attentive than other children to certain sights, touches, sounds or tastes. Sometimes this intense interest blocks out other stimulation for them and they become very absorbed.

Extension
Divide the circle of paper in two and invite the children to make mirror image patterns. Look for the mirror images in the kaleidoscopes, too.

LEARNING OBJECTIVES FOR ALL THE CHILDREN
● to recognize and explore how sounds can be changed
● to recognize repeated sounds and sound patterns.

INDIVIDUAL LEARNING TARGET
● to join in a social activity.

Bongo!

Group size
Six to 12 children.

What you need
A bongo drum or something to beat, such as upturned buckets, plastic containers, tambourines and empty boxes, for each child.

What to do
Sit down in a circle on the floor and place all the drums in the centre. First, teach the children a 'magic sign': when you raise your arms up high, all the children should stop what they are doing. Teach the children this chant:

> Bongo, bongo, play the bongo!
> If you're *(wearing blue)*, you can play the bongo!

In the second line, make the children stop and think of new words, for example, 'If you're wearing red', 'If you walked to nursery', 'If you're three years old' and so on. Help the children to think this through and encourage those who correspond to the description to come forwards and play a bongo drum in the centre. Raise your arms to quieten the children and ask them to sit back in the circle. Repeat three or four times, then choose a line that fits everyone, such as 'If you come to *(name of your group)*, you can play the bongo!'.

Now teach the children to echo your sound. Shout a word as you beat, and encourage a 'my turn, your turn' echo game, saying, for example, 'Hi!' (one beat), 'Bon-go!' (two beats), 'Bon-go-drum!' (three beats) and 'Bin-go-bon-go!' (four beats).

Special support
Ask a helper to sit with the child that you are targeting. Use a large drum such as a bodhran and give the child a beater. Ask the helper to hold it close to the child for the beat but to move it away at the end so that the child does not continue beating

indiscriminately. In this way, you are encouraging the turn-taking and allowing the child to hear the correct echo.

Extension
Challenge older children to beat the syllables of each child's name.

LINKS WITH HOME
Encourage parents and carers to play simple turn-taking games at home with card games, balls or echoes.

LEARNING OBJECTIVE FOR ALL THE CHILDREN
to respond in a variety of ways to what they see and feel.

INDIVIDUAL LEARNING TARGET
to work with a partner.

Slinky tricks

Group size
Two or three pairs of children.

What you need
A 'slinky' toy for each pair (stretchy spirals made of plastic or metal); large wooden blocks.

What to do
Gather the children around and show them the slinky toys. Show how they can be passed from one hand to another by placing one end flat in each palm, then raising one hand higher than the other. Use this opportunity to

encourage turn-taking between the children since there are twice as many children as slinky toys. Ask the children not to twist or stretch the slinky toys as they could be damaged.

Now, invite the children to each choose a partner and sit opposite each other on the floor. Show them how to hold on to one end of their slinky toy. Then chant or sing a rhyme as one child raises their end high, and the other low, see-sawing the highs and lows between them. For example, use this traditional nursery rhyme:

> See saw, Marjorie Daw,
> Johnny shall have a new master.
> He shall have but a penny a day
> Because he can't work any faster.

You could also use the rhyme 'Row, Row, Row Your Boat' (Traditional).

If you have a small flight of stairs or a low table available, demonstrate to the children how the slinky toys can be made to tumble.

Finish by encouraging the children to experiment with wooden blocks and the slinky toys in pairs. Support them as they try to make platforms and steps for their toys to tumble from.

Special support
Children who are severely affected by their autism need to develop simple reciprocal play. Slinky toys are an ideal way for an adult and child to interact together, as they are attractive to hold and to look at.

Extension
Challenge the older children to use their blocks to make simple flights of stairs to let their slinky toys fall down.

LINKS WITH HOME
Consider buying miniature slinky toys, which can be obtained very cheaply from market stalls and toyshops. Let the children take them home to enjoy with their parents and carers.

LEARNING OBJECTIVE FOR ALL THE CHILDREN
● to explore colour, form and sound.

INDIVIDUAL LEARNING TARGET
● to play reciprocally with a partner.

Rattling rollers

Group size
Four to six children.

What you need
Cardboard tubes and lids such as cardboard bottle packaging or drum-shaped containers; conkers; dried butter beans; large pasta shapes; scissors; Fablon or similar sticky covering.

What to do
Arrange the craft materials on the table. Show the children the drum-shaped containers and talk about their round shape. Place one or two conkers or beans inside one of the containers and put on the lid. Pass the container to one of the children and ask them to make a sound out of it. Take it in turns shaking it, tipping it and rolling it along the floor. Talk about the sounds that you make as you each experiment with the cylinders, trying different fillings to see which make  interesting noises when they are rolled. The children might suggest other suitable fillings.

When you are all happy that you each have a good rolling instrument, help the children to cover the surface of their cylinders with colourful covering such as Fablon, helping them to keep it smooth so that it still rolls. Experiment on a slight incline and compare the sounds that each finished cylinder makes.

Finish by playing a rolling game in pairs, asking each child to roll and rattle their musical toy to their partner. You can accompany yourselves by singing the rhyme 'Merrily We Roll Along' (Traditional) as you roll and return the instruments.

Special support
Rolling a musical cylinder is a good way of encouraging reciprocal play for a child who appears to 'be in a world of their own'. Work with the child that you are targeting, helping them to receive and push back the instrument to their partner.

Extension
With older children, introduce words to describe three-dimensional shapes, such as 'cylinder', 'cube' and 'cone'.

LINKS WITH HOME
Ask parents and carers to help their children to find at home containers that are 'cylinders'.

CREATIVE DEVELOPMENT · CREATIVE DEVELOPMENT · CREATIVE DEVELOPMENT

LEARNING OBJECTIVE FOR ALL THE CHILDREN
● to express and communicate their ideas using movement and music.

INDIVIDUAL LEARNING TARGETS
● to move with confidence in front of an audience
● to develop awareness that they are being watched and applauded.

LINKS WITH HOME
Ask parents and carers to play different styles of music for their children to move to and for them to watch and applaud.

Move it!

Group size
Ten to 20 children.

What you need
A large shaker; marimba or tambourine; selection of musical tapes or CDs; tape recorder or CD player; open space; clown or jester hat; adult helper.

What to do
Start by sitting in a circle together on the floor. Arrange for your helper to sit with the children while you stand in the centre of the circle. Explain that you are going to be a sad clown who cannot move. Put on the hat and stand floppily and dejectedly. While the children are still watching you curiously, arrange for your helper to pass the marimba to one of them and to encourage them to shake it. When you hear the shaker, move animatedly and face the player, dancing and smiling. Then 'freeze' again until another child is given a turn. After a few turns, some of the children might like a turn in the centre of the circle. At the end, ask all the children to find a space and 'freeze'. Play different clips of music for them to dance and move to, freezing again between the passages of music.

Special support
Children with autistic difficulties find it hard to understand that what they do has a consequence on other people. Ask the helper to focus the child's attention on the dancing clown while they are shaking their instrument, and to help them to start and stop their shaking, watching how the clown starts and stops, too.

Extension
Invite older children to design a piece of percussion music suitable for making the clown happy.

LEARNING OBJECTIVE FOR ALL THE CHILDREN
● to explore colour and form in two dimensions.

INDIVIDUAL LEARNING TARGET
● to work co-operatively with a partner.

Handy pairs

Group size
Two children at a time.

What you need
A roll of paper; washable coloured felt-tipped pens; glue; glitter; scissors; smooth floor surface.

What to do
Cut off pieces of paper from the roll. Help the children to each choose a partner and demonstrate how to draw around each other's hands on to the pieces of paper. Invite the children to take turns to draw so that each child draws their partner's right hand, then each draws the other's left hand. Praise them for taking turns.

Unroll the paper and ask one child to lie down on the floor next to the paper while the other child helps you to decide where to cut off the paper so that it is just longer than the lying child. Now ask the child on the floor to lie on top of the paper. Support the other child as they draw all around the body. When this is done, swap places so that each child has a turn at being drawn around.

Now have fun as each child fills in their own body and hand shapes, using the coloured felt-tipped pens, glue and glitter. Display the glittery handprints and body shapes to male a colourful wall frieze around the room.

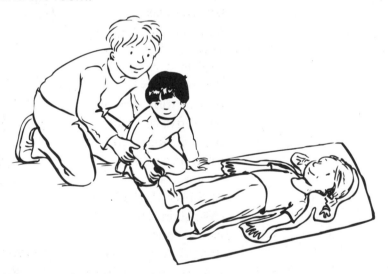

Special support
This activity is borrowed from 'relationship play', in which children become gradually more used to physical contact. The activity can also be used when working with the children and their parents or carers to improve their relationship and closeness. In this situation, the child is helped to draw around the adult lying on the floor, then the adult draws around the body of their child, who lies within their own contour.

Extension
Show the children how to turn glittery handprints into tropical fish or Christmas-tree designs.

LINKS WITH HOME
Suggest that parents and carers play a turn-taking game at home with their children, drawing around each other's hands.

LEARNING OBJECTIVE FOR ALL THE CHILDREN
● to use their imagination in dance.

INDIVIDUAL LEARNING TARGET
● to respond to 'Stop!', 'Go!' and 'Wait!' instructions.

LINKS WITH HOME
Ask parents and carers to point out familiar road and shop signs when they are travelling, and to teach their children to 'read' these.

Moved by music

Group size
Eight to 20 children.

What you need
Three sheets of A3 card, one with 'STOP' written on it in red, one with 'GO' written in green and the third with 'WAIT' written in orange (alternatively, use red, green and orange card with the words written in black); musical tape or CD; tape recorder or CD player; open space.

What to do
Encourage the children to wear pumps or trainers for this activity. Move to your open space and invite the children to find a space of their own and to sit down in it. Ask the children if they have noticed the traffic-lights on the roads when they are out with their parents or carers. What colours are the lights? What does each colour mean?

Show each of the cards in turn as the children call out the words. Now jumble them up and challenge the children to read them again.

Explain to the children that they should watch the cards carefully. Encourage them to stand up and have a few practices, stopping, waiting for instructions (such as 'Walk!', 'Jump!' or 'Crawl!'), then moving as you have suggested. Praise them for looking and listening well.

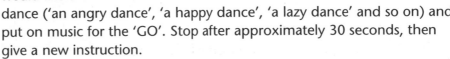

Now use the 'WAIT' card to tell the children how you would like them to dance ('an angry dance', 'a happy dance', 'a lazy dance' and so on) and put on music for the 'GO'. Stop after approximately 30 seconds, then give a new instruction.

Special support
A child who behaves as if they were 'in a world of their own' might be happy to help you to hold up the cards. Draw their attention to the fact that all the children are watching and doing what the card tells them, thereby showing them that their action led to a reaction from the rest of the group.

Extension
Ask older children to help you to think of new instructions.

LEARNING OBJECTIVE FOR ALL THE CHILDREN
● to design and make a mask.

INDIVIDUAL LEARNING TARGET
● to make eye contact when wearing a mask.

Magic masks

Group size
Three or four children.

What you need
Sheets of card; scissors; felt-tipped pens; paints; string or ribbon; tissue paper; collage materials; glue; table.

What to do
Arrange the craft materials on the table and invite the children to come and make masks. Explain to them that a mask does not have to represent anything or anyone in particular, and that they can make fantasy masks by applying a range of collage materials and leaving a space for the eyes.

Show the children some different effects such as fringing and crumpling pieces of tissue for shaggy, layered effects; using pasta patterns and bold painted stripes; adding cardboard noses or ears, and so on.

When the masks are complete, tie string or ribbon to small holes in the sides so that they can be tied on the children's heads. Some children might prefer to just hold theirs in front of their faces.

Special support
Some children are very frightened of masks and dressing up. Use the 'desensitization programme' on the photocopiable sheet on page 94 to help a child to overcome this anxiety step by small step. You are aiming to encourage the child to feel comfortable when looking at you in a mask, and also to feel able to wear a mask and look at themselves. Never tie the mask on and make sure that each stage stays relaxing and happy.

Extension
Invite older children to design a mask on paper, then try to make it with different materials.

LINKS WITH HOME
If necessary, explain the desensitization programme to parents and carers and advise them on how to use it effectively at home.

Individual education plan

Name:	Early Years Action/Action Plus

Nature of difficulty:

Action	Who will do what?
1 Seeking further information	
2 Seeking training or support	
3 Observations and assessments	

4 Encouraging social play and communication
What exactly is the new social/communication skill that we wish to teach?

How will we teach it?

What opportunities will we make for helping the child to generalize and practise this skill throughout the session?

How will we make sure that the child is fully included in the early years curriculum?

Help from parents or carers:

Targets for this term:

How will we measure whether we have achieved these?

Review meeting with parents or carers:

Who else to invite:

I like it!

Make a choice! What do you want to do next?

SPECIAL NEEDS **in the early years:** Autistic spectrum difficulties

Name it!

What is Teddy doing now?

Train game

Enjoy this chant with your child at home.

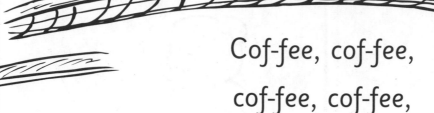

Cof-fee, cof-fee,

cof-fee, cof-fee,

Cheese and biscuits, cheese and biscuits,

cheese and biscuits, cheese and biscuits,

Chocolate pudding, chocolate pudding,

chocolate pudding, chocolate pudding,

Fish and chips, fish and chips,

fish and chips, fish and chips,

SOOOOOOOOOOOOOOUP!

Hannah Mortimer

Match the numbers!

8	1	7
6	4	2
3	9	5

Clock-face

Can you match the numbers at the bottom of the page with the ones on the clock? What time is it now?

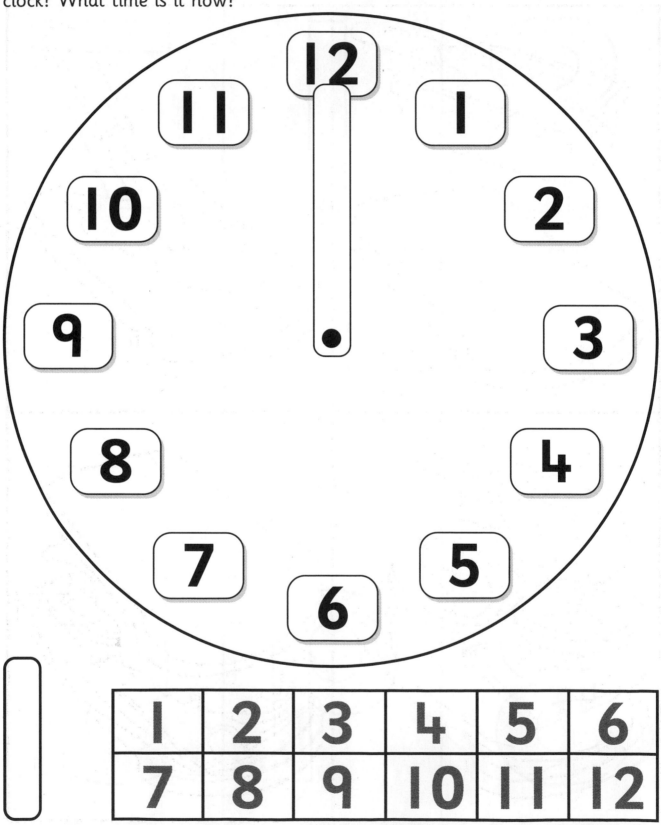

SPECIAL NEEDS in the early years: Autistic spectrum difficulties

Sandwich sequence

Can you make a sandwich?

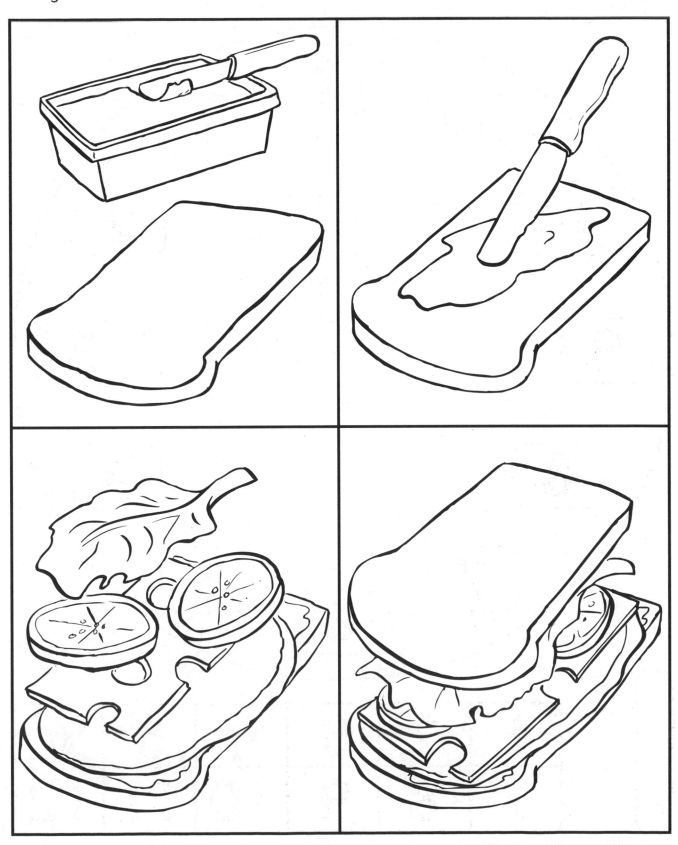

That's very odd!

Follow the leader

What instrument did you play today? Colour it in.

drum	harmonica	jingle bells
bongo	tambourine	Indian bells
cabasa	recorder	tulip block
wooden block	cymbals	guiro

Magic masks

Masks can be fun. Use these activities over several sessions for any child who is worried about masks and dressing up.

1 Get out your pens and paper. Design a paper hat for a teddy. Do not cut it out yet. Draw her lots of beautiful hats.

2 Cut out your hats and hold them in front of Teddy. Show her a mirror and let her admire herself.

3 Design a mask for Teddy. Do not cut it out yet.

4 Cut the mask out. Talk to Teddy gently as you place it on her.

5 Your teacher will draw faces. You add hats and beards. Make them look really funny. Show them to your parent or carer at home time.

6 Your teacher will draw faces. You make paper masks to cut out and put over them. Make some of them funny.

7 Your teacher will draw a big face all over the paper. You make a big mask and cut it out. Place it over and lift it off several times. See how funny it looks.

8 Make another big mask and cut it out. Make it beautiful, sparkly and funny. Put it in a closed box when you have finished.

9 Open the box and admire your beautiful mask. Find a big teddy bear to hold it against for a few seconds. Try it on all your cuddly toys, and tell them not to worry.

10 Hold the mask over your face and count 'One, two, three' slowly. Now hold it in front of your teacher (12 inches away) and count 'One, two, three' slowly. Put the mask back in the box.

11 Hold the mask against both your faces again but close up. Make funny noises. See who can be funniest.

12 Use your mask with the dressing-up hats, too. Look in the mirror for just a moment.

RECOMMENDED RESOURCES

ORGANIZATIONS AND SUPPORT GROUPS

● The *CaF Directory* of specific conditions and rare syndromes in children with their family support networks can be obtained on subscription from Contact a Family, 209–211 City Road, London EC1V 1JN. Tel: 020-76088700.

● The National Autistic Society, 393 City Road, London EC1V 1NG. Tel: 020-78332299.

● The Royal College of Speech and Language Therapists, 2 White Hart Yard, London SE1 1NX. Tel: 020-73781200.

BOOKS FOR ADULTS

● *Asperger Syndrome* by Cumine, Leach and Stevenson (David Fulton Publishers)

● *Circle Time for the Very Young* by Margaret Collins (Lucky Duck Publishing)

● *All Together: How to Create Inclusive Services for Disabled Children and Their Families* by Dickins and Denziloe (National Early Years Network)

● *Semantic-Pragmatic Language Disorder* by Charlotte Firth and Katherine Venkatesh (Speechmark Publishing, available through Winslow, tel: 0845-9211777)

● *Autism: Handle with Care* by Gail Gillingham (Winslow)

● *Special Needs and Early Years Provision* by Hannah Mortimer (Continuum)

● *Developing Individual Behaviour Plans in Early Years Settings* by Hannah Mortimer (National Association for Special Educational Needs). Available from NASEN, 4–5 Amber Business Village, Amber Close, Amington, Tamworth, Staffordshire B77 4RP. Tel: 01827-311500.

● *The Music Makers Approach: Inclusive Activities for Young Children with Special Educational Needs* by Hannah Mortimer (NASEN)

● *Autistic Spectrum Disorder: Positive Approaches for Teaching Children with ASD* by Diana Seach (NASEN)

● *What Works in Inclusive Education?* by Sebba and Sachdev (Barnardo's)

● *More Than Words: Helping Parents Promote Communication and Social Skills in Children with Autistic Spectrum Difficulties* by Fern Sussman (Hanen Centre Publication)

● *Children with Autism* by Trevarthen, Aitken, Despina and Roberts (Kingsley)

● *The Autistic Spectrum* by Lorna Wing (Constable)

BOOKS FOR CHILDREN

● *Russell Is Extra Special* by Charles Amenta III (Magination Press)

● *Little Rainman* by Karen Simmons (Winslow)

WEBSITES

● The Department for Education and Skills (DfES) (for parent information and

for Government circulars and advice including the SEN *Code of Practice*): www.dfee.gov.uk
● The Hanen Centre (parents' training and publications): www.hanen.org
● For information on the Lovaas Approach: www.icdl.com/lovaas.html
● MENCAP (support organization for children with severe learning difficulties and their families): www.mencap.org.uk
● The National Autistic Society : www.nas.org.uk
● PECS (Picture Exchange Communication System): www.pecs.org,uk
● The Writers' Press, USA (publish a number of books for young children about a range of SEN): www.writerspress.com

EQUIPMENT SUPPLIERS

● Acorn Educational Ltd, 32 Queen Eleanor Road, Geddington, Kettering, Northamptonshire NN14 1AY. Supply equipment and resources for early years and special needs.
● KCS, PO Box 700, Southampton SO17 1LQ. Specialist tools for making computer equipment accessible to all children.
● LDA, Primary and Special Needs catalogue, Duke Street, Wisbech, Cambridgeshire PE13 2AE. Tel: 01945-463441. Supply *Circle Time Kit* by Jenny Mosley (puppets, rainstick, magician's cloak and many props for making circle time more motivating).
● National Association of Toy and Leisure Libraries, 68 Churchway, London NW1 1LT. Tel: 020-73879592. Send sae to find out where the nearest toy library is. Also publish the 'Playsense' pack for play for babies and young children.

● Quality for Effective Development, The Rom Building, Eastern Avenue, Lichfield, Staffordshire WS13 6RN. Tel: 01543-416353. Supply *Playladders* (a checklist of play), *Starting Out* (a talk-through approach to prepare a child with SEN for a new school) and *Taking Part* (talking to a child about statutory assessment), all by Hannah Mortimer.
● Step by Step, Lee Fold, Hyde, Cheshire SK14 4LL. Tel: 0845-1252550. Supply toys for all special needs.

ORGANIZATIONS THAT PROVIDE TRAINING COURSES

● Children in Scotland, Princes House, 5 Shandwick Place, Edinburgh EH2 4RG. Tel: 0131-2288484. Courses in early years including SEN.
● EarlyBird Project, NAS EarlyBird Centre, 3 Victoria Crescent West, Barnsley, South Yorkshire S75 2AE. Tel: 01226-779218.
● I CAN Training Centre, 4 Dyer's Building, Holborn, London EC1N 2QP. Tel: 0870-0104066. Day courses for those working with language-impaired children from early years upwards.
● Makaton Vocabulary Development Project, 31 Firwood Drive, Camberley, Surrey GU15 3QD. Tel: 01276-671368. For information about Makaton sign vocabulary and training.
● National Association for Special Educational Needs (NASEN), address on page 95. Publications and workshops on all aspects of SEN.
● National Children's Bureau, 8 Wakley Street, London EC1V 7QE. Tel: 020-78436000. Seminars and workshops on children and SEN.
● National Early Years Network, 77 Holloway Road, London N7 8JZ. Tel: 020-76079573. Customized in-house training.
● National Portage Association, PO Box 3075, Yeovil, Somerset BA21 3JE. Tel: 01935-471641. For Portage parents and workers, and for training in Portage and information on the 'Quality Play' training.
● Pre-school Learning Alliance, Pre-school Learning Alliance National Centre, 69 Kings Cross Road, London WC1X 9LL. Tel: 020-78330991. Information on DPP courses and their special needs certificate. Free catalogue, order form and price list of publications also available.